VERTICAL GARDENS

VERTICAL GARDENS

Introduction by JACQUES LEENHARDT

Essays by ANNA LAMBERTINI

Principal Photography by MARIO CIAMPI

verbavolant

First published in the United States of America in 2007 by

Verba Volant Ltd.

Pellipar House, First Floor

9 Cloak Lane

London EC4R 2RU

Vertical Gardens was created and produced by Verba Volant Ltd.

verbavolant

e-mail: info@verbavolantbooks.com

website: www.verbavolantbooks.com

ISBN-10: 1-905216-07-6

ISBN-13: 978-1-905216-07-9

Introduction by Jacques Leenhardt

Translated from the French by Katy Hannan

Essays by Anna Lambertini

Translated from the Italian by Miriam Hurley

Pages 2–3: Quai Branly Museum Plant Wall, Paris (Jean Nouvel, Patrick Blanc)

Page 4: Xerox Brazil Building, sketch (Roberto Burle Marx)

Pages 8 and 240: Centre Commercial Quatre Temps Plant Wall, Paris (Patrick Blanc)

Pages 26–27: Prada Aoyama Epicenter, Tokyo (Herzog & de Meuron)

Printed in China by Sing Cheong Printing Co. Ltd.

INTRODUCTION

Jacques Leenhardt

The ficus and climbing plants had developed in an unvaryingly perpendicular direction, imposed by the density of the element which had produced them. Motionless, even after I had parted them with my hands, the plants immediately returned to their original position. This was the realm of verticality.

—Jules Verne, *Twenty Thousand Leagues Under the Sea*

Verticality

A garden appears first of all as a planted composition spread over the surface of a terrain bordered by a horizon. It is horizontal. It belongs to the large family that includes the landscape of endless fields that disappear in the horizon on the Beauce plain in France and the limitless open prairies of the American frontier. However, just as in our imagination the vertical silhouette of the Chartres Cathedral is essential to the landscape of the Beauce plain, and the enormous silos painted by Charles Demuth belong in the landscape of the American West; since ancient times verticality has been a fundamental element in the layout of a garden. Both landscapes and gardens are determined by the two axes we use to identify our position in the world.

Neither the ancient Greeks nor the Romans had a specific word for the garden. *Kepos* in Athens or *hortus* in Rome were used to describe what formed the boundary and protected a reserved private space. The garden was first defined by the tracing and boundaries of a reserved space within the immensity of an agricultural or untamed landscape. It was, and indeed still remains, the repetition of the idea of contriving culture within a natural area, a small crease or fold in the infinite woven fabric of nature. The horizon that surrounds it may be a wood, a forest, or the walls of a town. The horizon is the sign of verticality in the plane infinity.[1]

1. Though the "haha" plant does not obey the logic of verticality, the surprise (that gives the plant its common name) generated by the downward growth of the plant pays tribute to the idea of verticality.

9

[opposite] *Cabinet de treillage*, attributed to Jean Goujon (circa 1546).

One could follow the same line of reasoning when considering the natural character of a garden: an area composed of earth and rocks, enhanced with a variety of plants; when compared to our towns and houses, the garden is a space of untamed nature. And yet, because of its boundaries, and the care taken in its cultivation, the garden is a contrived space, from the very moment it is conceived, throughout its whole existence as a garden, before its eventual return to the state of wasteland. The flower beds, the fruit espaliers, the plant stakes, the marked out pathways—all these aspects show the presence of man who imposes a form that he likes to contemplate, which provides specific sensations as well as the fruits he likes to taste. The garden is fundamentally a cultural concept. It is obvious from this paradoxical form of introduction that the "vertical garden" on which we are focused here is in some ways redundant: all gardens are influenced by the verticality of the vegetation, and by the symbolic verticality that represents human intervention. This is not without some association with the fact that in the context of nature, man sees himself as a vertical element. "What walks on four legs, then two, and then three?" the Sphinx asked Oedipus.

"What image can we create which unites the common criteria of all mankind and their ancestors?" the anthropologist may ask himself, to which he replies, "the first and most important of all aspects is the upright position."[2] The mature adulthood of the human being is expressed by his verticality, the age where he has developed all his potential capacities; at this point of his life he is at the peak of his cycle, at the vertical apex of his human destiny. Despite this, our perception of the objects that are part of space in our world is rarely vertical. Cartographers and architects use plane vision, projecting at ninety degrees a vertical view down on the world. But this vision remains relatively abstract: one cannot easily walk around in a map. This is why the bird's eye view or prospective perspective, or axonometric view was invented; a fancy metaphor to express a point of view that looks down on reality without dominating it completely, that does not aim down on an object at right angles reducing its shadow to that of midday.

The roots of verticality are to be found in the principles of life itself. Through its relationship involving photosynthesis, the growth of vegetation is essentially determined by the search for light. It adopts the form of vertical growth. Among the varieties of plant life, those that best represent this upward thrusting action are without a doubt the herbaceous species which range from the alfalfa in our plowed fields to the bamboo in tropical forests. Bamboo is able to grow more than three feet a day (3.97 feet according to Lopez)[3] and can reach a total height of 115 feet. Generally speaking, this vertical vigor is symbolic of all plant life, and this has led to the variety of plant manipulation that gardeners have aspired to: tying, staking, and pruning.

2. André Leroi-Gourhan, *Le Geste et la Parole, Tome I*, Albin Michel Paris 1964, p. 323.

3 Oscar Hidalgo Lopez, *Bambú*, Cali, Colombia, 1974.

Architecture

Since ancient times the garden as an art form has been closely linked with the techniques that demonstrate the work that man has performed to wrest the area reserved as a garden from the common horizontal vision of the landscape. The Hanging Gardens of Babylon, built by Nebuchadnezzar II in the sixth century B.C., were considered one of the Seven Wonders of the World, and one of the most brilliant examples of creativity in ancient times. Already at that time, the aim was to impose botanic and aesthetic culture in a context that would not be simply the transposition of an aspect of nature, but on the contrary, as a concept that was entirely cultural. For example, certain plants did not belong to local native varieties, and therefore their inclusion represents considerable botanical knowledge and effort. It is known that Nebuchadnezzar had these gardens built to console his wife Amytis who was homesick for the garden paradise of her childhood. From its very conception this was the artificial construction of another world. The creation of a garden far away from its source and natural habitat, and recreating the same conditions on terraces in the heart of the city, emphasized the eminent role of man within the program of nature as a whole. The uprooting from original territory was to become the symbol of human intervention in a project. It was to become a form of recreation, a complement in addition to the work of God. In the domain of creating a garden, the artifice consists first of all of combining architecture with nature. The very first example is represented by the art of topiary, which the dictionary defines as a: "decorative technique in which garden trees and shrubs are clipped to create an architectural form."[4]

In addition, different architectonic artifices have made it possible to transfer plants as far as possible from their land of origin. Even in ancient history it was common practice to use supports to train vines and other plants. Vines were trained to climb along the branches of other trees. This practice is still used today in some areas of the Mediterranean, but it was not long before this natural support was abandoned in favor of a man-made structure, based on pillars or columns, such as the pergola, which is depicted on the walls of the Villa of Fannius Sinistor in Pompeii.[5]

The development of bowers[6] and arbors follow the same principle. Originally, an arbor consisted of a support for a vine, high enough to enable people to walk underneath. Pliny the Younger described how it was possible to stroll barefooted under the delicious shade of the arbor at his country residence near Ostia. Diderot recalls this pleasant function of the arbor "to enjoy the freshness in the midst of a summer's day."[7] There are few documented references on the evolution of these techniques between the Roman period and the Middle Ages. It was not until the fourteenth century that documented examples appeared in Europe showing the development of

[opposite] *Pergola Italienne*, J.C. Nicolas Forestier (1920).

4. Alain Rey, *Le Robert, Dictionnaire culturel en langue française*, Paris 2005.

5. Pierre Grimal, *Les Jardins romains*, Paris, Fayard 1984, p. 247, p. 283.

6. Berceau or bower: arched arbor, covered with vegetation under which it is possible to walk. A style developed in French and Dutch gardens between the sixteenth and eighteenth centuries.

7. Diderot et d'Alambert, *L'Encyclopédie*, entry for *treille*.

gardens and the landscape. The book *Très Riches Heures du Duc de Berry*, by the Limbourg brothers, shows that trellises were used in Paris in the fifteenth century. From that period on, a distinction must be made between the two types of arbor: natural and artificial. In the gardens of the stately homes, the willow and wicker which were most commonly used as a natural support were gradually replaced by wooden or iron structures able to sustain a variety of decorative plants in constructions that were becoming progressively more and more sophisticated in style. Very often these structures, which became an important feature in the gardens of Versailles, were not covered with plants, and their role was to recall the idea of architecture within the garden space.

From this moment the history of verticality within the garden depended on the intrinsic capacities of the plants themselves as well as the artifices employed to encourage them to abandon the soil—source of their nourishment. Following the initial concept of the Hanging Gardens of Babylon, gardens began to include containers of varying sizes able to hold bouquets of flowers and other plants. This represented a kind of continuity of logic between the hanging garden and the flowerpot. This may seem an absurd comparison, but in both cases the fundamental action was the uprooting of the plant from its natural support: the earth. This symbolic meaning naturally led to the creation of the pot itself, followed by the flower box or planter, a remarkable object, to sustain the idea of the artifice. Surely it is no coincidence that the well known artist Jean-Pierre Raynaud, influenced by horticulture, has introduced the form of the common flowerpot as an icon of contemporary art.

We must distinguish between the support and the substrate. Natural soil provides both aspects at the same time. From the moment where this unified element is divided to remove the plant from the nourishment of the soil, we must deal with the question of humidity and the nutritive substances the plant requires. This is a question that Hector Horeau faced at the beginning of the nineteenth century at the time when the development of metal architecture led to the possibility of designing structures that were both lightweight and transparent. In his project to cover the boulevards in Paris, he thought of enhancing the very high glass roofing covering the pavements, by installing containers filled with soil to be planted with flowers that would cascade elegantly from above. Horeau did not ignore the question of the water supply and even designed a rainwater collector system for distribution according to the needs of each type of plant. The installation of these suspended hanging planters has become a popular solution used by many of those involved in urban decoration, because far from representing a love of the artifice, the system is a clever subterfuge destined to protect the plants from vandalism and damage caused by stray dogs.

l'Entrée du Salon de treillage au Jardin de M. Le Comte de Morstein à Montrouge

[top] *Entrée du Salon de Treillage de M. le Comte de Morstein à Montrouge*, Guilbert (circa 1650).

[above] *Pavillon de Treillage* in the gardens of the Sanssouci Palace in Potsdam.

[top] *1000 pots bétonnés peints pour une serre ancienne*, at the Domaine de Kerguéhennec Contemporary Art Center, Jean-Pierre Raynaud (1986).

[above] *Vue de l'Infiorata, École Pratique du Conservatoire*, Hector Horeau (1868).

8. Patrick Blanc, *Biologie des plantes de sous-bois tropicaux*, Université Pierre et Marie Curie, Paris 1989.

Botany

Up to this point we have discussed the plant and the art of manipulating its qualities in order to form a barrier, enclose an area or create a perspective in a garden. However, we must keep in mind that a garden is as horizontal as it is vertical, and in the same way, the roots that are hidden from view are just as important as the plant structure we have before our eyes. It is important to address the roots when contemplating verticality.

In botany, plant life is divided into two main categories according to the degree of visibility of their process of reproduction: phanerogams and cryptogams. The latter are plants in which the opposition between ascending and descending organs, roots, vegetation, nutritive function, and growth, remains uncertain to a large extent. Cryptogams include mosses, seaweeds, ferns, fungi, and, for those plants which are composed of one or several cells, even bacteria. A large part of these plants grow in areas with little or no light. The layering of plants in the vertical space of a tropical forest leads to considering the correlation of horizontal grouping according to their affinity in adapting to the particular conditions of an environment.

The principles that led Patrick Blanc to the creation of his *mur végétal* or vertical garden are deeply rooted in his studies of the undergrowth in tropical forests.[8] It seems a paradox that his interest in the ground level was renewed by his experience gained as a biologist studying the forest canopy. It is true that the canopy and the undergrowth form a complex system, and the expertise in this area has made an incredible leap forward thanks to the expeditions conducted in recent decades. Even the term "canopy" is recent and is linked with a radical change in opinion. Before, the spreading cover of the tree crowns as imagined from below was referred to as "forest roof." It was not until botanist observers were able to rise above the treetops that they discovered the existence of a canopy containing an infinitely rich biological world that was impossible to imagine from the ground. The canopy raft was invented by botanist Francis Hallé in collaboration with the architect Gilles Ebersolt and pilot Dany Cleyet-Marrel to study the forest canopy. The raft is a roughly seven hundred square yard inflatable platform that floats at treetop level, suspended from a one hundred fifty-foot-long hot air balloon. The first experiments were in French Guiana in 1996, then in Gabon (1999), in Madagascar (2001), and in Panama (2003–04). These airborne explorations played an extremely important role in learning about the problems that affect the survival of the tropical forest. Thanks to the information collected from the canopy, Francis Hallé was able to set up a widespread campaign to make the public aware of the dangers that threaten the

[left] *Crystal Palace, London,* Joseph Paxton
(1855).

Amazon forests and the predictable consequences for the regeneration of the earth's atmosphere.
The expedition led to discoveries that were so unexpected and images that were so spectacular
that the public became fascinated and rushed to discover this new floristic continent of incredible
beauty.[9]

Covered by a dense canopy, a dome-shaped layer formed by the leaves on branches and creepers that have entwined around the branches and trunks for support, the tropical forest lets only a
very small part of the light filter through, sometimes only a little over one percent. The plants that
grow in layers under the canopy have had to develop systems in order to survive in conditions that
are not very favorable for photosynthesis. Given the conditions to which they have become accus-
tomed, these plants in the undergrowth do not attempt to capture more light by rising higher. They

9. Patrick Blanc, *Être plante à l'ombre des forêts tropicales,*

Nathan, Paris, 2002.

occupy the space between ground level and a height of about sixteen inches. A tiny percentage may sometimes reach as high as six feet. The area between the undergrowth and the canopy is mainly occupied by epiphytes or plants that cling to trunks and branches of the tall trees in the tropical forest, feeding on their sap (parasites) or on the remains of fallen leaves that have accumulated in bark crevices. Here, biological reservoirs are formed where single cell lichens, moss and algae can grow and gradually form mounds of plant residue on the branches that will feed the large epiphyte varieties such as philodendrons, bromeliaceous species or ferns. In a natural manner, these nutritional reserves accumulated at considerable height were the harbingers for the substrates that were to be used later for vertical gardens or green walls in urban contexts.

Vegetation in the Urban Context

Urban centers today are currently searching for areas to plant vegetation in order to transform the carbon dioxide produced by traffic and heating into carbon hydrates and oxygen. Real estate speculation makes it extremely difficult to find the space necessary for green areas. The intensity of this problem differs according to the type of city—the old European style urban structures like Berlin, London, and Paris, as opposed to the more recently developed cities like New York, São Paolo, and Shanghai. The urbanism of the garden-cities inspired by Ebenezer Howard[10] has indeed left irregular traces in various urban structures, and certain large industrial sites that have been abandoned are now being converted to create new green parks, like the Parc Citroën in Paris and the IBA Emscher Park in the Ruhr region of Germany. This also applies to operations aimed at converting railway lines no longer used into green corridors, like the *coulée verte* in Paris, or covering an urban motorway with planted gardens.[11] However in an urban context these solutions sometimes require a large amount of space. In the seventies, as part of the legacy of Frank Lloyd Wright and in strong contrast to modern trends at the time, a new movement called "green architecture" began to appear. The main figures of this movement remain James Wines and Emilio Ambasz. It consisted of developing a form of architecture integrating a strong element of plastic arts that focussed very strongly on the ecological aspect, referred to as "site." This notion gave its name first to a publication, and later to an architectural group. SITE developed its contacts with artists such as Nancy Holt, Robert Smithson, Alice Aycock, Vito Acconci, and Gordon Matta-Clark, with architects as different as Robert Venturi, Peter Cook, Gianni Pettena, and Emilio Ambasz, as well as with groups like Coop-Himmelblau in Vienna, and Antfarm in Toronto.[12] The main aspect

10. Ebenezer Howard, *Garden-Cities of To-morrow*, London 1902.

11. Designed by Michel Corajoud and built in Seine-Saint-Denis, in Paris.

12. James Wines, "A Short History of the Beginnings of SITE, 1969–77," in *SITE*, Rizzoli International Publications, New York, 1989.

that stands out in the work by Wines and the SITE group during this period is their research into solutions able to modify the dominant representative aspects of architecture. These provocative projects fully justified their existence, as with the well-known *High Rise of Homes* (1981), which proposed a vertical structure where each story was composed of a dozen small houses, each one with a different style and with its own private garden. This idea of "verticalizing" village-style architecture was echoed twenty years later in the Flower Tower by Edouard François; this time the project was actually constructed. The project gave each home conditions that were comparable to those of a small house surrounded by its own garden.

From the point of view of providing inhabitants with the impression of living in the country, vertical architecture presents an undeniable advantage since theoretically the system can be multiplied almost without limit throughout a city.

Originally, the technical idea of the *mur végétal* or vertical garden was based on both the fact that certain plants like epiphytes and parasites already present in natural habitats did not depend on the soil, and the fact that this autonomy could be applied to urban contexts, or more generally, to architecture. Roberto Burle Marx is the first landscape artist to have put these principles into practice. Three factors played a deciding role to permit Burle Marx the application of this innovation. The first concerns ecology. Burle Marx worked in a country very strongly influenced by its position between the equator and the tropic of Capricorn. In the 1930s he began designing gardens aimed at replacing imported European flora with native plants. Based on research carried out by botanists and explorers, he worked to discover a large number of new species, which were then named after him. Burle Marx expanded the choice of plants available for gardeners and at the same time he "Brazilianized" or "tropicalized" his gardens. In particular the bromeliaceous species caught his attention, together with a large number of saxicole varieties that grew on the granite rocks in the region of Rio de Janeiro where he created many of his gardens. The project developed by the ecologist José Lutzenberger for Guarita Park (1973–78), located on a rocky cliff face overlooking the sea near Torres, Brazil, combined on vertical surfaces certain plant species that need only the small amount of nourishment found in rock crevices and sea mist.

The second deciding factor was the abundant presence of epiphytes, orchids, and bromeliaceous varieties in the tropical forests. These plants are parasites that cling to a vegetal structure that provides sufficient nourishment. Burle Marx exploited the aesthetic possibilities available using these climbers in the park he designed for the University of Florianópolis, where

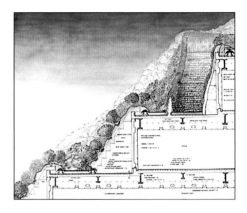

[above] Section of the ACROS Building, Emilio Ambasz (1997).

[opposite] *High Rise of Homes*, James Wines (1981).

he recreated an exemplary biotope based on an environment of fern species. The third factor that led Burle Marx to imagine the concept of vertical gardens was based on his close working relationship with architecture. In the 1930s Burle Marx worked on a project with Lucio Costa and Le Corbusier and created a hanging garden for the Ministry of Health and Education in Rio de Janeiro. His frequent collaboration with architects, Oscar Niemeyer in particular, led him to create a large number of gardens that often had no access to natural soil. This was the case for the Safra Bank project in São Paolo. Burle Marx built a garden on an upper floor, almost completely composed of mineral material, in strong contrast to the planted columns and "vegetal" wall panels. A deciding factor in the success of this type of artifice is the ability to apply knowledge and experience in epiphyte plant biology to manage the substrate where the plants feed and grow. Burle Marx collected and applied thick panels of fern roots (*Dicksonia sellowiana*) to the walls on which he planted bromeliaceous varieties. He used the same technique to erect plant columns which also included epiphytes.

With these innovative interventions Burle Marx paved the way for the use of vertical gardens in urban contexts with a favorable, humid, climate. These innovations applied to the concept of planting in the urban space were later developed in two main directions. During the sixties many artists were influenced by the emerging problems concerning ecology. While "earthworks" and "land art" began to enter the North American artistic conscience, in Buenos Aires Luis Benedit invented the *Phytotron*, a hydroponic greenhouse where the principles of cybernetics created a metaphor of the nature cycle. With the increase in vast urbanization and galloping pollution rates, artists became more sensitive to the endangered environment. One example, in an action that could be considered a militant provocation, was the Canadian artist Francine Larivée's attempt to introduce vegetation into a museum—a rash undertaking since the ecological conditions that existed within the walls consecrated to cultural heritage were deadly for the mosses that the artist wanted to present in the exhibition. Conscious of the contradiction, the artist re-oriented her work toward the concept of not presenting the mosses themselves but instead exhibiting the conditions necessary for their survival. Working in collaboration with biologists, she created in an artificial habitat the equivalent of a biotope, a new form of art to be exhibited in a museum.[13] This led to further collaborations and integrations of the advances made in biology into the world of art. Botany and art merged to create new uses for plants outside their natural habitat and research into new nourishing substrates allowed artists to erect vertical gardens for the dual purpose of aesthetics and ecology.

[top] Parque da Guarita, Torres, Santa Catarina, Brazil, José Lutzenberger (1973–78).
[above] Plant columns, Safra Bank Headquarters, São Paolo, Brazil, Roberto Burle Marx (1983).

13. Francine Larivée collaborated with several Canadian botanists and with Claude Figureau, the Director of the Jardin des Plantes in Nantes, in order to use to best advantage Figureau's research into substrates enabling vegetation to be grown away from the soil.

[top] Trunk with epiphytes, campus of the University of Florianópolis, Brazil, Roberto Burle Marx (1982).

[above] Plant panel, Safra Bank Headquarters, São Paolo, Brazil, Roberto Burle Marx (1983).

The Aesthetics of Vertical Gardens

A green or plant wall constitutes a particular facet of verticality in garden art. It has the unusual characteristic of being developed separately from a garden in areas that have no natural green context. It is an urban and architectural element. The examples presented in this book immediately demonstrate how well a vertical garden is able to improve the grayness of concrete architecture. The population density of cities causes their inhabitants to endeavor to bring a little touch of "nature" and color into their homes in the midst of an overwhelmingly mineral environment. Flowered balconies, the proliferation of plants in the home, the rising success enjoyed by gardening centers offering a wide variety of plants, and the green spaces being developed in built-up areas are all proof that this is a trend in expansion.

If one considers the current trend for vertical gardens it is apparent that, in its own way, it entails the same aesthetic features belonging to traditional art forms such as drawing, painting, and sculpture. Drawing and painting are echoed in the treatment of the surface plane of the image. The first imposes a line, and the second the form and color. Terunobu Fujimori's Tsubaki Castle has plants that follow, and emphasize, the lines of the structure. Grass strips contrast with the various materials used in the building. It is only when one is quite close to the work that it is possible to identify individual plants. From a distance the plants seem to form a visual grid, rather like a page from a notebook. Fujimori follows the same theme in his Grass House where the planting on the walls and roof follow the lines of the structure imposed by external materials, in this case stone.

The pictorial effect of the planting on the walls is far more striking in the works by Patrick Blanc. One has the impression that the gardener, or botanist (or perhaps we should simply call him the artist), varies the textures, density, and tones of the plant material in the same way as if the wall were a classical painting. Chardin and Millet often worked their oil pigments emphasizing the thickness and texture. They spread paint "with a trowel," as it is sometimes called, applying paint as if it were mortar. At the same time these same artists, and others like them, tried to give an impression of fluidity to their pigments and to deepen the subtle art of transparency. The most talented, like the painter Pourbus, overlaid a fine gossamer glaze to create the illusion of volume without sacrificing the single dimension of the canvas. It seems that Patrick Blanc has rediscovered the science of the old masters by the careful selection of the species he uses. Certain plant walls seem to have a landscape quality, or perhaps that of an abstract work where different spaces are arranged to catch light and reflect a huge variety of images. This is no plain green surface, but an art form of chromatic and symphonic harmony.

The surface of the wall to which the plants are applied is exactly like the canvas on which the artist makes his brush marks. A fern drops its long plumed fronds against an almost unbroken background of the tiniest leaves; a cascade of broad streaks in different colors provides movement and rhythm over the entire surface; in the midst of a myriad of greens, suddenly a glimpse of red appears recalling the flower garlands of "Velvet" Breughel. Patrick Blanc has an artist's palette of foliage available: from the tender greens cascading in delicate mist, to the striking contrast of sharp spiky grasses that explode against the background like slashes of acid. The subtle mixture of effects and harmonizing of forms and shades over the surface of the plant walls are beyond description but this infinite assortment attracts our curiosity to discover the diversity of the foliage in detail.

Foliage in the Art of Tapestry

Rather than limit ourselves to a comparison with painting, perhaps it is more fitting to look more closely at the strong similarities between these shimmering green walls and the art of tapestry weaving. Historically, at least since the fifteenth century, the art of tapestry has been devoted to plant motifs, aristolochia, and other floral offspring. Having undergone a veritable revolution in recent decades, the quality and texture of the materials become even more important; now available are wools, cottons, and silks, but also animal hair, natural plant fibers, metal wire, and every type of weave generated by wickerwork and braiding throughout history. This artistic revolution has transformed the ancient medium of tapestry into a contemporary art form which has ceased to be considered an auxiliary to painting (one of the lesser arts) and to be classified as a form of handcraft. Leaping away from the restrictions of the floor or the wall and developing into an independent volume in space, tapestry became a new form of art far closer to sculpture. By detaching itself from the planar surface of the wall, contemporary tapestry has jostled the traditional barrier between a painting and a piece of sculpture. With their work, artists like Sheila Hicks or Olga de Amaral have launched a new genre where the texture of the fiber is able to assume all its artistic importance, where the yarns and elements used in the weave are no longer subordinate to color and form.

[opposite, from top to bottom]

Fitotron, Luis F. Benedit (1973).

Enfouissement de traces, Francine Larivée (1994).

Mousses en situation, Francine Larivée (1983).

Offrande, Francine Larivée (1990).

The same occurs with the *mur végétal*. Although it also offers a variety of chromatic effects, the vertical garden makes far more use of texture, transparency, and contrasts between materials and densities. The foliage is arranged to create tightly packed effects alongside loose flowing tendrils, like hair blowing in the wind, shimmering in the play of shadow and light. In other areas, there are dark masses, gleaming vibrant leaves that absorb the daylight and hollow out a visual abyss in the surface.

In works of art of this kind, superb notes spring forth that have never existed in the world of painted art. This is made possible by the fact that the vegetation exists in total liberty in a space free of any support from a wall. There are combinations of techniques that offer the possibility to escape the architectural limits imposed by walls. In Parking des Ternes, a collaboration between Edouard François and Patrick Blanc, the vegetation occupies a central space and does not depend on walls for support. Entwined tresses of foliage cascade down through a void left by a stairwell as it crosses through the various parking levels. This long vegetal structure flows like a waterfall; endless variations of every shade of green play with the vibrant prism of colors that identify each floor of the garage. The effect is absolutely enchanting. One has the impression of a gigantic plant suspended in an underwater universe like the floating seaweed in Jules Verne's *Twenty Thousand Leagues Under the Sea*. This green life force, which seems to burst forth from an abyss in the center of the earth, amazes and delights those who discover it; the lighting has been designed to eliminate the dreary dimness that one normally finds in buildings of this kind. In the depths of this well-ordered green cavern, inspired by the charm of this pure artificiality, images of mysterious cave life spring to mind.

There is little doubt that the concept of the *mur végétal* most resembles sculpture in the *cheminée végétale*, fruit of another collaboration between Edouard François and Patrick Blanc. Unlike the majority of Patrick Blanc's work designed for interiors, where the lack of daylight dictates a choice of plants that do not require much light, the *cheminée végétale* is outside. It is located in a square in the heart of La Défense, a remarkable area because of the quality of its glass architecture and the height of its buildings. In this context, the artist decided to use climbing plants to great effect; they harmonize particularly well with the dominating verticality of the urban space. Instead of cascading down from a support base, hundreds of plants climb training stakes arranged in an upward slanting direction around a chimney. The creepers are *Ipomea convolvulus* rooted in copper planters spiked with hundreds of chestnut wood climbing stakes. From a distance it almost seems like a pale stubby cypress tree thrusting hundreds of branches toward the sky.

In Flower Tower by Edouard François we find the same principle using a single foliage throughout. The balustrade that encloses the balconies on each floor of this apartment building is interrupted frequently in random sections by large white concrete flower planters set into the structure itself. This forms a decorative linear border of truncated cones which the architect has filled with bamboo plants. This creates a very light and airy effect giving movement to the structural elements of the façade. Since they have grown well, the bamboo bow their heads with nonchalance now that they have reached the balcony of the floor above, delicately disturbing the linearity of the façade. From inside, the inhabitants catch a glimpse of the world through a delicate leafy curtain creating the exotic impression of a world in constant transformation.

It seems that this green movement has been adopted on an international scale. Each botanical or architectural tradition will create its own unique solutions. The projects are still predominantly done in the key of experimentation but this provides for an exciting diversity of new proposals. One fact remains certain: ecological well-being, long a concern for garden designers and landscape artists, has become an issue for architects as well. Urbanists have taken up the challenge, and collaborative projects are emerging among various professions that have too often been compartmentalized in the past, leading to renewed outlooks and emotions. The city and its inhabitants cannot help but benefit from this movement. There is something in the air, and the vogue for green walls is a positive sign.

TREE TENANTS
VIENNA

Hundertwasser

[opposite] Detail of Hundertwasser House, seen from the corner of Löwengasse and Kegelgasse in central Vienna.

Friedensreich Hundertwasser was a provocative and controversial artist. He forged an original path in art and design following the principles of his own particular naturalist theory based on the simple premise that "nature is an end in itself. It has no other cause than itself. Nothing exists outside of it. The perfect autocracy of its structure generates universal harmony, beauty. Art is the path that leads to beauty." (Pierre Restany, 1997). For Hundertwasser the assertion of a naturalist aesthetic, in which the rules of nature govern the rules of art, meant defending the beauty of curves and spirals against the "tyranny of the godless and immoral straight line." This was an obvious attack on the modernist culture of International Style and rationalism in architecture, against which Hundertwasser made his deep-rooted hatred clear. Based on these ethical suppositions, Hundertwasser focused his theoretical and artistic pursuits on the need to enact—first on an individual level and then on a collective level—an everyday reconciliation between art, technology, and nature. He worked passionately on a plan for an aesthetic-naturalist society and on inventing a new poetic quality for living spaces.

Hundertwasser's entire artistic production rests on a philosophical corpus articulated in his many public speeches and dogmatic manifestos. With his 1958 *Mold Manifesto against Rationalism in Architecture*, he styled his rejection of rationalist architecture, laying the foundations of his naturalist theory. The manifesto extols the freedom of building and, inspired by mold (a material that swells rigid surfaces through slow progressive proliferation), offers a metaphor for asserting a

new strategy for dwelling and for the idea of an architecture based on the use of soft fluid lines. His first nude speech against rationalism in architecture dates to 1967 at the Hartman Gallery in Munich where Hundertwasser greeted guests "as God made him." For Hundertwasser, literally baring himself was a means of elucidating one of his particular cultural positions—that people have three skins: the epidermis, clothing, and a house. Ridding oneself of the second skin allows the first skin to assert its right to a proper third skin. With the passage of time and the maturation of his work Hundertwasser came to recognize a fourth skin, social identity and its context, and a fifth, the environment on a global scale.

When the celebrated 1908 essay *Ornament and Crime* by Adolf Loos was republished in 1968, Hundertwasser published his manifesto *Loose from Loos* in which he restated his assertion of the people's right to exercise their natural creativity in the places where they live. In 1972 he published another dogmatic text, *Your Window Right—Your Tree Duty,* coinciding with an important shift in ideology: defending the choice to plant trees inside houses. The premise is that when plant life passes through the window it is sure to bring an improvement in the quality of the environment and to serve as an effective anti-pollution device, thereby serving tenants and city dwellers. Addressing the later directly, Hundertwasser stated, "it is your right to design your windows and, as far as your arm can reach, your outside walls just as it suits you." Furthermore he declared that "free nature must grow wherever snow and rain fall, everything white in winter has to be green in

[above] The multi-hued façades of Hundertwasser House.

[above] Hundertwasser House, seen from above. Tenant trees colonize the roof and balconies.

summer. Everything horizontal under the open sky belongs to nature. Roads and roofs should be planted with trees. It must be possible to breathe forest air in the city again."

At the 1973 Triennale di Milano, Hundertwasser presented his project for tree tenants, planting twelve trees in the windows of the nineteenth century façade of the Grand Hotel et de Milan on Via Manzoni. The underlying concept is that tree tenants help to recreate a balance in urban environments where rainwater is unable to penetrate the cement and asphalt cover. Tree tenants turn the floors of buildings into fertile ground, purify water and thereby pay their rent. This was such an appealing idea to the artist that he introduced it into various projects and perfected construction techniques for its implementation. The tree tenant theme stretches from his first projects for architectural hygiene to the redesign of building façades such as the Rosenthal factory in Selb and the Rupertinum Museum in Salzburg where trees grow across the windows and shapely tongues of colored ceramics decorate the window ledges. In 1986 the public opening of the Hundertwasser House in Vienna—with its bizarre colored façades and more than two hundred trees and bushes on balconies, terraces, and rooftops—introduced the public to a wider notion of green architecture as the symbiotic integration of plant life and building.

PARK UP A BUILDING
SANTIAGO DE COMPOSTELA

Vito Acconci

[opposite] Park visitors sit on the suspended benches of Vito Acconci's ingenious *Park Up A Building* in Santiago de Compostela.

In 1996 a unique suspended structure was attached to the Alvaro Siza designed Centro Gallego de Arte Contemporanea museum complex in Santiago de Compostela. It was a prototype of *Park Up A Building*, an ingenuous design by New York-based artist Vito Acconci to convert the unadorned walls of a building into usable public space. Vito Acconci began making experimental works in the sixties and his oeuvre includes performance, installation, and video art, as well as designs for urban art and architectural projects. In 1988 he founded Acconci Studio, an innovative laboratory of urban art production that employs an interdisciplinary group of designers. Among the unique spaces generated by Acconci's design think tank are Storefront for Art and Architecture in New York (a cultural and exhibition center, the fruit of a partnership with the architect Steven Holl), an artificial island on the Mur River in Graz, Austria (which holds a theater, café, and playground), and a store for the Museum für Angewandte Kunst in Vienna.

Park Up A Building is one of many projects by Acconci that applies aesthetic principles to public space. Given that the primary scope of these projects is the creation of a realm that fosters social life and the activities of ordinary people, the design approach is not necessarily inclined toward investigating possible structures; instead it is focused fostering the creation of a space that can accommodate changes in use and social meaning over time. Its creators describe *Park Up A Building* as a portable park, a hanging modular structure that adapts to any kind of blank wall and that can be adjusted to variable heights. The system can be installed permanently or temporarily and is composed of telescoping aluminum tubes, modular grates, trees with burlap sacks of earth, and fluorescent lights. These elements can all be combined to make two different hanging modules, which can be used alone or combined. One module has seats on two sides. The other has seats on the inside and trees on the outside. As the modules are joined to each other steps and landings are formed. According to the studio "the floor, the seat, and the step are metal grating—you can look up through them; the tree is enclosed within a metal grate, its roots encased in the burlap sack it was transported in. A light from beneath each floor illuminates the park. Each successive module is hung one step higher than the one before: as you walk through the park—as you walk from step to floor, between seat and seat and between seat and tree—you're climbing up the side of the building." Though these trees with their roots in the air might be a bit bewildering, the overall effect is that of a benevolent parasitic structure with the impermanent look of a construction site. It plays with the possibility of transforming the wasted walls of host buildings into usable space for recreation. This idea was recently revisited and developed in a study of new options for introducing plant life in cities by Gilles Clément for the APUR (L'Atelier parisien d'urbanisme) in Paris.

[opposite] Occupying a smooth wall of Alvaro Siza's Centro Gallego de Arte Contemporanea, the park is supported by eighteen L-shaped steel beams that descend from the roof.

HIGH RISE OF TREES
ATLANTA

Vito Acconci

[opposite] *High Rise of Trees* is a multifunctional piece of urban furnishing conceived as a tree-lined sculpture-tower.

One of the many projects built in Atlanta for the 1996 Olympic Games was an original multifunctional piece of urban furnishing by Vito Acconci. *High Rise of Trees* was a steel pole tower structure that held a series of small trees arranged one on top of the other, vertical landscaping as orderly as it was unique. Each tree was planted in a clear Plexiglas pyramid-shaped container. A semicircular bench at the base allowed the structure to serve as a resting spot for passersby. During the Olympics the tree tower also served as a route marker along a wide pedestrian thoroughfare made by temporarily closing a road connecting the Olympic stadium to suburbs of Atlanta. The importance of the tree tower as a point of orientation and as a landmark in the city landscape was further asserted, day and night, by spotlights built into the structure. It is difficult to categorize *High Rise of Trees*; it is a work that falls somewhere between environmental sculpture and urban furnishing. It was an unexpected piece that played with the rules of nature, making the most of the vertical dimension and suggesting new ideas for including plant life in cities.

DILSTON GROVE, LIFE DRAWING, GREEN BRICK GREEN BACK
LONDON, RIGA, HOUSTON

Heather Ackroyd, Dan Harvey

[opposite] "After years of searching for a church in London we were drawn to the deconsecrated religious site of the former Clare College Mission at Dilston Grove. We were curious about how the architectural space, the atmosphere, and the perceptions of people entering into it, would be affected by the application of our materials." (Heather Ackroyd, Dan Harvey, 2003).

For a few weeks in 1993 the façade of an eighteenth-century building in Zurich was covered with a thick green pelt of grass. Applied manually, germinating grass seed was planted into a thin clay substrate. In 2003, the same treatment was given to the interior of Dilston Grove, an old deconsecrated church in London. A small mausoleum in a ruined cemetery in Riga looked as if it had been absorbed by nature when it was covered in the same grassy composition for several weeks in 2004. For nearly two decades the English artists Heather Ackroyd and Dan Harvey have been working together on temporary installations that use grass as an aesthetic material. Exploring the use of seedling grass as a medium for art have led the pair to experiment with various processes for imprinting photographic images on grass surfaces to make temporary organic photographs. "In the greater body of our artwork we play with many materials exploring processes of growth, transformation, and decay, and we embrace the transience and ephemeral nature of our materials. Yet somehow the fragility of these chlorophyll apparitions urged us to make moves to preserve them longer." (Heather Ackroyd, Dan Harvey, 2001). By managing the process of chlorophyll production a gradient scale, comparable to a gray scale, can be created with the yellow and green of sprouting grass. The early impressed light-sensitive images remained intact only for short periods of time and were easily altered by too much or too little light. To further develop their work, Heather Ackroyd and Dan Harvey have drawn on the scientific support of researchers at IGER, Institute of Grassland and Environmental Research, in Wales. "These sci-

entists have developed a grass that keeps its green even under stress. In a naturally occurring variant of grass, they identified a gene for a protein that degrades the green pigment chlorophyll, and by modulating the expression of this gene, they were able to alter the grasses' aging behavior and even stop it altogether. Through a plant breeding program they have introduced this trait, coined a stay-green, into a rye grass. The application of this grass in our work has subsequently led us to grow photographic canvases and then dry them. While the green blades retain their chlorophyll much more effectively than regular grass, the effects of other processes, such as oxidative bleaching, gradually occur and over time contribute to an irreversible loss of image." (Heather Ackroyd, Dan Harvey, 2001). The system of creating a photographic image with a vertically grown carpet of seedling grass was utilized in the 2004 installation *Green Brick Green Back* at the Rice University Gallery in Houston, Texas. The walls in the exhibition space were covered with vertical fields of grass, set with images of a brick wall and the back of a U.S. one dollar bill.

[above] A grassy pelt grows on the vertical plane turning the space into a verdant green chamber.

[opposite] Photographic images of U.S. one dollar bills from *Green Brick Green Back* installation at the Rice University Gallery, Houston.

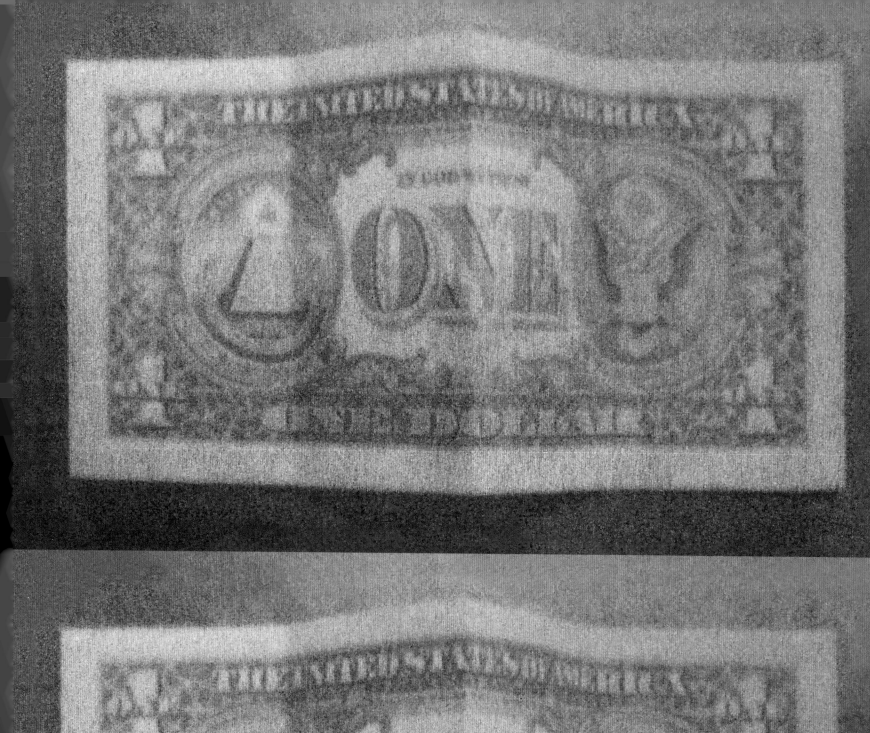

[above and opposite] A small neoclassical
mausoleum in a cemetery in Riga, Latvia
was covered with a mixture of grass seed,
mud, and water to create the work *Life
Drawing*.

PUPPY
BILBAO

Jeff Koons

[opposite] Jeff Koons's floral sculpture *Puppy* sits at the entrance to the Guggenheim Museum in Bilbao.

Puppy is a big passive West Highland White Terrier puppy, eleven and a half meters high, made of a steel and wood substructure completely covered by a multicolored layer of small annual plants. Held to be American artist Jeff Koons's most popular work, the unique sculpture was exhibited for the first time in 1992 in the courtyard of the Arolsen Castle near Kassel and was later acquired by the Solomon R. Guggenheim Foundation. Since 1997 it has made its permanent home in front of the entrance to the Guggenheim Museum in Bilbao. The surreal jumbo-sized toy was conceived by Koons "as a symbol of love, warmth, and happiness." *Puppy* draws on kitsch strategies to elicit intense sentimentalism in observers to whom, in a confusion of the senses, the piece might appear "simultaneously minuscule and gigantic. It is a glorification, simultaneously repetitive and majestically unique, of the archetypical symbol of recognized beauty: the flower." (Terence Riley, 1994). The sculpture's monumental quality, rather than causing the disorientation normally associated with perceiving giant forms and objects, is absorbed by the sense of mawkish softness conveyed by the image represented. *Puppy* manages to affect viewers on the pervasive and explicit level of the aesthetics of communication. By using massive floral decoration and reproducing the features of a stuffed animal, the work stimulates simple affective sensations. It works with the most common figures of the contemporary collective image bank and manipulates them using the sort of advertising strategies that are capable of creating false needs and selling useless goods. On this point, Koons himself has noted that he tried to make a work that would make everyone, regardless of

where they are from, react and think, in one way or another, "I like it." This is the intent of *Puppy*, a garden sculpture decorated with seventy thousand plants; it is even equipped with an automatic watering system. Evocations of a gardening tradition founded on the use of elaborate floral decorations—such as seventeenth- and eighteenth-century *parterres de fleurs,* or decorations made by applying a horticultural technique at the peak of style in nineteenth-century gardens, "mosaiculture"—resonate within *Puppy's* contemporary neo-pop aesthetic.

With every changing season, the piece presents a new plant coat with shrilly bright multi-hued blooms in the summer and spring. In *Puppy*, the traditional flowering *parterres* designed to exalt the glory of royal homes take on a three-dimensional corporality, playing a duet in their unique aesthetic and material connection with the liquid architecture of the shining titanium-clad museum complex designed by Frank Gehry.

[above and opposite] *Puppy* is a playful, three-dimensional version of a traditional flower parterre, displaying seasonal multi-hued covering of varied annual and perennial herbaceous plants.

PARKING DES TERNES
PARIS

Edouard François, Patrick Blanc

[opposite] Columns of vegetation populate a Parisian parking garage with colonies of ferns, ficus, and other tropical plants.

According to architect Edouard François, the philosophy behind his redesign of Parking des Ternes entails rendering the "grand characteristics of the existing site" coherent. François wanted to develop a simple, inexpensive, and durable design solution that takes the end users into account. The five-level garage (with fourteen hundred parking places) is located under the Avenue des Ternes in the seventeenth *arrondissement* of Paris. Each level of this architectural void was converted into a rich single colored volume flooded with colored light. A succession of yellow, green, orange, blue, and red light has turned the parking lot into a multi-layered realm of colors. Empty spaces for infrastructure have been transformed into odd stagings of depth, in which we can physically immerse ourselves, passing through windowed stairwells arranged like surreal underground tropical greenhouses.

Inside each greenhouse, or stairwell, is a hydroponic cultivation system developed by Patrick Blanc that allows compositions of philodendrons, ficus, peperomia, creepers, and other tropical plant species to grow on the surfaces of the fifty-foot tall cement pillars that stand between the base of the lowest parking level and top of the highest. These plants have adapted to living in extreme conditions and obtain the light and heat they need from a system of carefully arranged spotlights. If a spotlight does not work correctly, parts of the plant system may be lost. Without careful maintenance, the plants will inevitably die and the botanical scene would become ghostly. The high temperatures and humidity in these botanical caves—these kingdoms of verticality—can

make it difficult for visitors to walk up and down the stairways. This sets the stage for an exchange of courtesies between people and plants, forced together in an environment that tests their vital relationship. The smell of mildew and moist plant life, the sound of drops of condensed water falling to the ground, the intense heat, the dense atmosphere in the large glass spaces, the sight of a sequence of colored lights—bring those willing to linger on a landing of one of the greenhouse-stairwells into a bizarre dimension of suspended time. After learning that Edouard François is related to Jules Verne, one cannot help but link the experience of a visit to Parking des Ternes with the fantastic places described in Verne's visionary novels *Twenty Thousand Leagues Under the Sea* and *Journey to the Center of the Earth*.

[above and opposite] The plant cladding on the columns creates an otherworldly atmosphere. The stairwells have been transformed into unexpected underground greenhouses.

[overleaf] From the stairwells it is possible to see the different colors of light (yellow, green, orange, blue, and red) that correspond to the five parking levels.

CHEMINÉE VÉGÉTALE LA DÉFENSE
PARIS

Edouard François, Patrick Blanc

[opposite] The forms and figures of the urban landscape in the La Défense district of Paris provide a contrasting background for the *cheminée végétale* or plant chimney.

At the base of the Coeur Défense skyscraper in Paris stands a nearly sixty-foot high cement ventilation tower for an underground parking garage. The tower is clad with plant life and introduces a horticultural element uncommon in this predominantly cement-covered office district. A joint project by architect and landscape designer Edouard François and botanist Patrick Blanc, the unique installation takes a piece of infrastructure and turns it into an urban landmark. The ventilation tower was turned a container for a botanical garden by wrapping the cement structure with thick panels that serve as flower basins. The full height of the cylinder is encircled with basins, angled bands of copper, and randomly placed chestnut wood stakes that jut out like a strange prickly armor. Various moonflowers, climbing plants of the *Convolvulaceae* family, were given homes in the flower basins and made to grow along the stakes.

The tower, with its sequence of stacked cultivated layers, is reminiscent of traditional terrace farming. Its leafy, bristling silhouette is a clever example of urban camouflaging. Here plant matter is used for more than banal decorative or screening purposes; it is a structural element in a hybrid architecture, changing with the passage of time and seasons. Moonflowers with their heart-shaped leaves and blooms in various shades of pink, lilac, and blue are not solely a variegated covering on reinforced cement; they transform an element infrastructure into a cultivatable and aesthetic space and thereby change the tower's figurative and semantic value. Late July to September is the best time to admire the tower's blooms. The plants utilized are only a sampling of the more than

three hundred species, cultivated under the scientific guidance of Patrick Blanc, in the arboretum of the Parc de la Vallée aux Loups in Chatenay-Malabry. The autumnal show displayed by the *cheminée végétale* is equally poetic; the leaves and petals that cover the tower fall to the ground and form spirals on the concrete pavement.

[above and opposite] François and Blanc have turned an unremarkable cement column into a verdant sculpture. The *cheminée végétale* translates the ideas of site-specific art installations into a skillful urban camouflaging project.

[left and opposite] The design of the tower makes use of organic and inorganic materials. The cladding serves as a container for a collection of morning glory plants.
[overleaf] The autumnal version of the color and texture of the plant composition.

GÎTES RURAUX
JUPILLES

Edouard François, Duncan Lewis

[opposite] Trees are utilized as a façade. The appeal of this architectural invention rests on a paradox: a natural image is achieved by forcing trees into an artificial shape.

Gîtes ruraux are hospitality facilities to accommodate travelers and vacationers longing for nature. "Farm holidays" have become very popular in France and other European countries in recent years. In response to the growing demand for a countryside escape, a network of farms, old houses, and rural centers throughout France have been converted for tourism. The design of one hospitality complex near Jupilles, a small town in the Loire Valley on the edge of the Bercé forest, is based on a concept of integrating architectural elements with the surrounding landscape. The architects, Edouard François and Duncan Lewis, decided that "the answers are around us, not in us." Certainly a refuge that resembles a tree house, instead of vacation apartments, on the edge of an oak forest is a rural getaway.

The project is a collection of camouflaged apartments set within the context of landscaping for a converted farm complex. The exteriors of seven cement and wood structures are hidden by the branches of newly planted trees. These branches form a continuous plant façade, held in place by metal fences and forced into a sort of topiary form, bringing to mind the linear precision of classic French garden palisades. The use of diverse species of trees, including evergreens and deciduous trees, results in a composite pattern of forms, colors, and densities. The project has a paradoxical architecture—it uses natural materials and seeks to blend into the landscape, but it also bends and forces trees into rigid forms, subjecting nature to the rules of artifice. This enchanting botanical and architectural sculpture evokes archaic myths that speak to the symbolic, magical value attrib-

uted to the vertical nature of trees which, since ancient times, have been held to be a source of life and a link between the earth and the heavens. The work draws from the history of the art of garden making and a wide repertoire of figures and creations of hybrid furnishings designed and built with arboreal structures. For example, in the sixteenth-century Parco di Pratolino designed by Bernardo Buontalenti for Francesco de Medici, there was an inhabitable tree described in archival documents as "an oak tree of inordinate size whose top is reached on two leaf covered ladders, above which there is a space of sixteen connected branches bound by places to sit with a table, in the middle of which springs a crystal-clear fountain."

[above and opposite] Architecture at the edge of an ancient forest; Jupilles' *gites ruraux* are camouflaged to blend in with the landscape.

[overleaf] The *gites ruraux* complex seen from the oak forest.

[left and opposite] A sequence of the architectural solids (the residential units) and architectural voids (outdoor spaces for picnicking and recreation) have been inserted within the tree-lined enclosure.

[overleaf] Evergreen and deciduous species make up the façades of these vacation houses. The tree branches are aligned by a wide metal mesh fencing.

PRADA AOYAMA EPICENTER
TOKYO

Herzog & de Meuron

[opposite] The play of volumes in the open space surrounding the Prada Aoyama Epicenter in Tokyo.

Prada chose to locate its second flagship store in the Aoyama district of Tokyo. The aptly named Epicenter serves as an architectural manifesto of the brand, made to impress consumers and forge a point of attraction. In these new designer label meccas, where shopping is rendered an exclusive experience for privileged customers, making a high profile architectural impression is more important than mere retail function. Flagship stores are meant to become new focal points in the urban landscape. In Tokyo—where the streets are unnamed and orientation relies on visual experience and constructing impalpable mental maps—the Prada Aoyama Epicenter has become a community icon, a powerful visual point of reference that helps those moving through Tokyo not to get lost.

The small six-story tower designed by Herzog & de Meuron, termed a "crystal with a few sharp edges," is a visionary and sensual structure that opens toward the city on each side with transparent façades of convex and concave rhomboid glass modules. The architect notes that: "We thought about glass, but not the glass of modernism, of Mies van der Rohe, which is always flat: this glass is convex, concave or flat, each part selected in relation to the human eye. The result is an optical machine, that attracts or distances the gaze, casting light or shadow on the products." (Jacques Herzog, 2003). The building develops upward and leaves a small section of the lot free. Shaped into a flagstone rock garden, this void is charged with a visual function: to isolate and make legible the shifting contours of the glass tower. The space is bounded by a low architec-

tural dune clad with curving dark gray stone slabs hosting a delicate carpet of natural moss. This border defines a small open space where the transparency and reflections of the sculpted glass blocks of the tower generate the illusory impression of verticality. It is a vertical garden at the ground level.

[above] The small, refined empty space complements the glass tower. The depth of the border wall contains utility spaces.

[opposite] Detail of the wall cladding; a soft moss grows on its surface.

KEMPINSKI HOTEL ATRIUM
MUNICH

Helmut Jahn, Peter Walker

[opposite] The atrium of Kempinski Hotel in Munich is an unusual greenhouse garden where artificial nature is cultivated.

The Kempinski Hotel in Munich is an integral part of a new airport complex built in the early nineties on the northwest edge of the city. The hotel's figurative central point, the atrium, is the result of a collaboration between German architect Helmut Jahn, creator of the complex, and American landscape architect Peter Walker who was asked to design the open spaces. The fusion of Walker's minimalist forms and the grandiose transparency of Jahn's architecture resulted in an enormous glazed envelope that encloses a surreal, cartoon-like greenhouse garden. It seems as if the 15,000 square-foot atrium was designed as an entrance to an indoor garden that encompasses the building.

In the atrium of the hotel, a space that brings to mind an airplane hangar, the concept of a garden as a place where nature is cultivated for aesthetic purposes is evoked in an ambiguous manner. This "garden" plays with a combination of faux natural elements and actual plants. Twenty-foot high transparent walls of square glass panes supported by steel frames divide the atrium in two, separating a lounge area from the reception. A sequence of walls traces a path across the atrium and follows a line of pink and gray granite and marble slabs in the floor that continues outside after passing under the atrium's high glass walls. The visual effect, enhanced by the play of reflections from the various glazed surfaces, is to erase the separation between inside and outside, a visual merging of the interior of the building and the outdoor park. Plastic red geraniums in pots are placed in groups of three in rows along shelves attached to walls. Two circular compositions of

artificial palm trees mark the café area. These soaring palm trees introduce a note of lounge-style exoticism while the rows of repeating faux geraniums on the modular shelves act as a parody of the orderly flowered balconies found along Bavarian streets.

The outside space adjacent to the atrium has a traditional system of trellises in the form of wooden pyramid-shaped structures, planted (not always successfully) with English ivy. These elements are meticulously integrated into precise geometric divisions that govern the design of the entire hotel. At night, the atrium is lit by suffused green and blue lights that underscore the atmosphere of an artificial oasis suspended in a dimension of travel.

[above and opposite] The high greenhouse-style walls, with orderly rows of vases with plastic geraniums, are positioned both inside and outside forming geometric partitions.

[overleaf] Transparency and reflection are components of the design.

[second overleaf, right] View toward the hotel's internal courtyard.

[second overleaf, left] Detail of the high glass walls with vases of faux geraniums.

FONDATION CARTIER PLANT WALL
PARIS

Jean Nouvel, Patrick Blanc

[opposite] In addition to a botanical panel by Patrick Blanc, the entrance of Fondation Cartier boasts multi-colored pavement and a large flowerpot by Alessandro Mendini.

The living botanical tableau above the entrance to the Fondation Cartier in Paris is the first true meeting between Jean Nouvel's architecture and Patrick Blanc's plant walls. In 1998 the director of the foundation, Hervé Chandès, invited Blanc to participate in the Etre Nature exhibition. Blanc proposed building a vertical garden facing the interior entrance hall, and a corresponding plant wall on the exterior of the building above the doorway. With Nouvel's approval, the garden was realized and the external portion remained after the exhibition closed. Before the addition of this garden into the Fondation Cartier, Blanc had designed a plant wall for a Nouvel project for the French embassy in Berlin. But the Berlin project did not go forward and consequently the Fondation Cartier garden became the first Blanc plant wall to be built in a Nouvel construction. Even though the plant wall was not part of the building's original design, it immediately forged a favorable relationship with the façade, becoming an essential part of the entrance rather than a simple decorative panel.

The Fondation Cartier was completed in 1994 and is considered to be one of Nouvel's most important works. The architectural design is based on transparency and seeks to create spaces of light. The use of glass as the main construction material is a tool for implementing a well defined strategy for erasing form. The design of the building and its external spaces takes into account the surrounding context which includes a neighborhood park and a symbolic cedar tree planted by the French poet Chateaubriand in the early nineteenth century. The result is a simple yet sophisticated spatial organization defined by parallel planes of glass screens. Aligned with the boulevard that runs in front of the Fondation, these screen walls provide a backdrop for the grand cedar. The concept of mimetic architecture, a structure conceived as a conceptual extension of what we see, shaped a building where "in the summer, the large sliding windows disappear, and the room becomes an extension of the park, paced by tall columns. ...from the boulevard, the building looks like a halo, with the sky as a background, superimposed on the trees, whether real or virtual, trees reflected and refracted by the glass backdrops.... It is a building made of lightness, glass and thin steel, a building that plays with the possibility of blurring the structure's tangible limits and making its interpretation as a solid volume superfluous in the poetic of the "*flou*"[blur] of evanescence, in a building that allows the neighborhood to enjoy the sight of a beautiful, long hidden garden." (Jean Nouvel, 1994).

This introduces a kind of aesthetics of evanescence, a "Phantom of the Park" as Nouvel himself describes the project. This expression clarifies the meaning of a work that seeks to evoke a sense of place and involve the architecture in the setting for which it was made. Through the constant movement of transparencies and light, the smooth and reflective large glazed surfaces enhance the visual dynamics tied to the building's use and its surrounding urban landscape. Looking toward the façade, it is easy to confuse the direct view of the sky and that seen in transparency between the real and reflected trees. The vertical garden exuberantly takes part in this visual dance of the multiplying views and overlapping of real and virtual images, forming, on the lightweight, transparent façade, a wedge of solid, porous, and verdant surface, impenetrable to light.

[opposite] The play of transparencies and reflections on the building's large glazed façades creates real and reflected images.

PARC FLORAL PLANT WALL
PARIS

Patrick Blanc

[opposite] Parc Floral's plant wall is composed of a variety of carpeting and shrub plants.

Park Floral was designed in 1969 by French landscape architect Daniel Collin as a space for horticultural and botanical themed exhibitions. The plant walls added by Patrick Blanc are one of the botanist's first projects in the public sphere. Commissioned by the park and garden service in Paris, the plant walls are intended to demonstrate the possibility of cultivating vertical spaces to the public.

Blanc's vertical gardens are inspired by the growth and adaptation strategies of plants native to tropical forests. As a botanist and researcher for CNRS (*Centre national de la recherche scientifique*), Blanc spent years engaged in devoted study and participated in several scientific expeditions. During his journeys to Cameroon and French Guiana he spent months observing tropical canopies (the highest part of the forest) from platform laboratories built on treetops one hundred feet above the ground. Taking cues from plants that have the ability to live in a very small amount of earth, Blanc developed a system for cultivating vertical gardens. The considerable number of botanical species adapted to this type of cultivation allows for the creation of endless varieties of living compositions, all with different textures, colors, scents, and patterns.

In the eighties Blanc adopted the principles of hydroponics (which allow plants to grow in nutrient solutions) and began experimenting—using the walls of his own home as a testing ground—with materials and structures that would make this type of cultivation feasible on an inexpensive basis. The result of Blanc's work is a simple yet ingenious and fully patented vertical

garden system. Compact non-woven synthetic felt (roughly a quarter-inch thick and able to absorb water and retain a certain amount of water) is spread on rigid PVC sheets and attached to steel frames. A system of frames can be free-standing or anchored to the interior or exterior walls of a building leaving a gap to avoid water infiltration. Plants are then inserted into special pockets in the felt where they are cultivated. The compactness of the planting depends on the growth needs and physical features of each species, but generally the planting density ranges from twenty to thirty small plants per square yard. The plants' environment is kept moist by an automatic drop-by-drop irrigation system that delivers water enriched with minerals. A timer governs the watering intervals, regulated according to both the requirements of the plants and the climatic and environmental conditions. Finally, a basin is placed at the base of the wall to collect the excess water and return it into circulation in the distribution system after it is filtered.

[above and opposite] One of the pavilions of Parc Floral contains an educational exhibit with Patrick Blanc's plant walls.

[overleaf, left] Nutrient enriched water is circulated through the plant wall and collected in the basin that surrounds the free-standing panel.

[overleaf, right] A detail of the "educational" plant wall reveals its rich botanical composition which includes *Nephrolepsis cordifolia, Philodendron pertusum, Platicerium* sp., *Ficus* sp.

PERSHING HALL HOTEL PLANT WALL
PARIS

Andrée Putman, Patrick Blanc

[opposite] Balconies that overlook the internal courtyard of the Pershing Hall Hotel command an excellent view of Patrick Blanc's creation.

A sophisticated restoration turned a nineteenth-century building, which once served as a head-quarters for the United States during World War I, into one of the most exclusive hotels in Paris. The interior design was executed by one of the world's most prestigious designers, Andrée Putman, who penned the interior of the Concorde. For the Pershing Hall Hotel, a short walk from the Champs Elysées, Putman created an elegant setting that takes the building's history into account. The exotic vertical garden by Patrick Blanc covering one of the walls facing the interior courtyard was part of the overall renovation plan and is the hotel's most visually appeal-ing feature.

This plant wall is the first large-scale implementation of Blanc's system, which had previously only been applied to relatively small portions of vertical space. Stretching nearly one hundred feet in height, the wall is a verdant living composition that spans the building's six stories. It remains one of the tallest plant walls completed by the French botanist and it turns the atrium into a fan-ciful primitive world, evoking a tropical plant-covered cliff. In the evening, fiber optics set among the plants form narrow luminous bands and the garden-courtyard takes on the atmosphere of an enchanting theater set.

Blanc's botanical composition includes an abundance of unconventional combinations with a number of exotic plants alongside more common garden plants. Carpet species like the *Vinca sp.*, *Cotoneaster sp.*, *Ceanothus sp.*, common grasses, and ornamental shrubs like hydrangeas, hostas, buddleia, deutzia, and cistus all fit perfectly with ferns, ficus, and peperomia. Blanc does not consider using climbing plants, which he feels are too invasive and complicated to manage in these kinds of compositions. Three hundred sixty species have been arranged to form a natural fabric with a variegated design. Blanc tends to configure his plant walls with bushes that have pattern-making hanging branches placed in higher sections and small herbage in the lower areas to create a more compact, delicate covering.

An inspiring example of beneficial cohabitation of plant species with different physical characteristics and biological needs is described by Patrick Blanc in his book *Le bonheur d'être plante* (*The Well-Being of Plants*). Speaking for a little Sonerila plant he writes of its "little friends along the edge of a stream" who "instead of seeing some species displace and eventually eliminate others by towering over them, they choose gentle cohabitation, blooming at the same level. Finally, it is nice to occupy the same environment together." He continues, "it is when the resources for abundant expansion are limited, and habitable spaces are separated from one another in time and space, that biodiversity can express itself fully, even in small spaces. Competition no longer has a place".

In Blanc's philosophy, the concept of advantageous cohabitation between living beings with different biological needs extends to the desire to foster a closer connection between city dwellers and elements of nature, including producing new artificial nature as seen in the design of plant walls.

[opposite] The plant wall creates an appealing, timeless atmosphere in the courtyard of the Parisian hotel.

[left and opposite] All of the spaces
that overlook the courtyard take part in
the exotic exuberance of the botanical
backdrop.

[overleaf] Patrick Blanc's plant wall
dominates the space of the covered indoor
courtyard.

[second overleaf] The verdant setting
brings to mind the fantastic jungles painted
by Henri Rousseau, exotic scenery for a
sophisticated hotel restaurant.

GENOA AQUARIUM PLANT WALL
GENOA

Renzo Piano, Patrick Blanc

[opposite] To survive in interior spaces plant walls must receive light from specially designed systems.

The Genoa Aquarium was built during Expo 1992 and was opened to the public in 1993. It is currently the largest aquarium in Europe. The structure was designed by Renzo Piano and covers four stories, two of which are below sea level. There are seventy theme-based tanks, exhibits that present not only fish and sea creatures but also aquatic flora and fauna from around the planet. Located at the end of an exhibit on the marine environments of Madagascar, near a crocodile pool, is a luxuriant plant wall made with Patrick Blanc's signature assortment of tropical species.

According to Blanc, aquariums were one of his passions when he was young and he looked after several of them at a time. His experiments with the care and maintenance of these small closed ecosystems were the starting point of his plant wall concept. "I had read in a German magazine that you should put a philodendron root in the aquarium to purify the water of all the waste substances, and I noticed that the philodendron thrived in the water without anything else. So, my first interest was water purification rather than creating plant walls. My philodendra started to grow and cover the walls of my parents' house right above the aquarium. This is why I tried to take out the water and make it run along the plants' roots and make it go back in the aquarium, forming a kind of closed circuit. When I was nineteen years old and I was at university, I went to Malaysia and Thailand for the first time to see for myself the plants that grew in the forest. Here I could see how plant life invaded everywhere, areas in the shade as well as branches and rocks. I knew that many plant species, like orchids and ferns, grew on branches, but I didn't realize that some of

them could even root themselves on rocks and that rocks in rainforests were completely covered. I then understood that I might be able to recreate the same conditions at home." (Patrick Blanc, December 2006). A boy's curiosity and a passion for nature, and a simple hobby around the house were the start of a rigorous course of research. It was the beginning of one of the most innovative expressions of the art of contemporary gardens.

[above] Blanc created a luxuriant botanical backdrop for the interior of the Genoa Aquarium.

[opposite] An incredible variety of shapes, colors, and textures can be found in Patrick Blanc's creations; he makes use of his extensive knowledge of the plant life to incorporate tropical species in the design of his plant walls.

CENTRE COMMERCIAL QUATRE TEMPS PLANT WALL
PARIS

Patrick Blanc

[opposite] A multi-hued weave with a rich botanical palette including a few common ornamental plants like guelder roses, geraniums, ferns, cotoneaster, and hydrangea.

Along a large pedestrian esplanade in La Défense there is a recess between two building fronts that allows one to catch a glimpse of a spectacular vegetal presence. Like the nearby *cheminée végétale*, the plant wall on the façade of the Quatre Temps shopping center is a rare instance of cultivated nature found along the emblematic grand axis of this quarter. Located on the western edge of Paris, La Défense has grown sporadically since the fifties and has become an international hub for the service industry. It has a concrete urban landscape, and its shining towers of steel, concrete, and glass speak the diverse, slightly arrogant, language of urban modernization in postmodern times. For Patrick Blanc, who does not try to hide his ambition to grow vertical gardens alongside skyscrapers (and in the heart of the suburbs), La Défense is a frontier to be conquered, "I have always loved the city. All I want is to bring nature outside the subway stop." The plant wall for Quatre Temps is part of a larger program for renovating the shopping center, which was originally opened in the early eighties and introduced as the largest in Europe. In an urban context marked with signs of globalization, the plant wall seems to serve as a curiosity, an independent point of attraction, an attempt to add value to a fluid place dedicated to the rituals of shopping. Working with a botanical mix that includes elephant ears, ficus, ferns, dieffenbachias, hydrangeas, and hostas, Blanc created a multi-hued composite texture, a sequence of diagonal waves. The effect is one of a dense, heavily embroidered textile. It is a living tapestry spread beautifully next to one of the shopping mall's entrances advertising the advantage of widespread use of plant life in cities.

[above] Detail of the upper portion of the plant wall.

[opposite] Like a sumptuous decorated fabric, this plant wall was designed with a wavy diagonal pattern, enhancing its ornamental effect. Patrick Blanc ensures that his creations will last at least thirty years.

[overleaf] These details show the variety of textures and nuances of color that Blanc is able to achieve by mixing botanical species.

MARCHÉ DES HALLES PLANT WALL
AVIGNON

Patrick Blanc

[opposite] Positioned like a billboard above the heads of passersby, the large plant wall in Avignon faces a square.

A one hundred-foot long and nearly forty-foot high plant wall dominates the north façade of a covered market in Avignon. The commission for the project, which cost a total of six hundred thousand euros, was given to Patrick Blanc by Avignon's public administration with the hope of bolstering the appeal of the city's historic center. Certainly a plant wall, particularly one of such substantial proportions, is a spectacular sight that could easily become part of a tourist itinerary.

The botanical palette that Blanc chose for this project turned the building's inorganic façade into a scenic living tableau, softening the rigidity of the simple architectural volume. The rich multi-colored design adds a facet to the building that is able to reflect daily and seasonal temporality and insert exotic connotations into the urban landscape. Patrick Blanc has stated that his "plant walls came out of a wish to bring a bit of exotic and unique verticality into our homes and our cities. And from the wish to create unexpected green areas in the midst of the asphalt and cement. Because these plant walls do not cover horizontal space, they can be put everywhere, even in the most congested metropolis." For Blanc the plant wall is much more than an original decoration or urban furnishing project; it is an opportunity to add natural material to the city, and increase the amount of chlorophyll and biomass in the built world. There are many well known environmental advantages of putting green coverings on urban facades including improving the microclimate, bettering the ratio of inorganic to organic mass, hydrothermal control, forming filters for dust, mitigating air pollution, and making microhabitats for birds and microfauna. These benefits are augmented

by the improvement to the visual quality of an urban environment beautified by widespread plant life. The plant walls designed by Blanc open up exciting frontiers for introducing a new category of urban greenery, whose greatest risk for now seems to be exhausting its innovative content in favor of merely masking ugly façades and banal building cover-ups.

[above] A view of the market square with its outsize, multi-colored backdrop.

[opposite] The plant wall was commissioned by the city administration as an urban improvement project.

[overleaf] Details of the complex array of botanical species that give life to the plant wall of covered market of Avignon.

VALUE TEAM HEADQUARTERS PLANT WALL
MILAN

Giacomo De Amicis, Ivana Porfiri, Luca Rogora

[opposite] The continuous plant wall, located in a stairwell, rises to a height of sixty-five feet.

The Milanese headquarters of Value Team (an Italian consulting and information technology company in the Value Partners Group) is organized in three blocks brought together by a subtle mixing of architectural volumes. Architects Giacomo De Amicis and Ivana Porfiri explain that "the presence of green areas and abundant natural light, as a structuring element for the building, goes along with the desire to create continuity between the interior and exterior of the building, challenging the boundaries of the container and causing the space to be perceived as being deeper than it actually is. A winter garden, a plant wall, plant roofs, patios, and greenhouses are positioned so that nature is a constant presence. They act as focal points as one passes through the interior, punctuating the architectural composition and forming a common thread. Natural light is allowed in from every possible angle to make the interior spaces luminous and alive."

The building is a white monolith that rests on a shining stainless steel clad base. A regular pattern of windows marked by bright orange frames helps define the architectural image that immediately identifies the structure. The principle façade of the complex is interrupted by a central incision made by the insertion of the entrance. The base of a twelve-foot wide plant wall, which develops to a height of sixty-five feet in the void of the stairwell, is located in the entrance foyer. Openly inspired by compositions of Patrick Blanc, the plant wall for the Value Team headquarters was designed by Luca Rogora who applied the technical skills and experience he gained while designing green roofs and components for the German company Optigrün Technology. His construction system for interior plant coverings consists of modular metal elements. Each module is a six-by-twelve-foot rectangle of tight mesh with a two-inch thick polystyrene panel for insulation attached on one side, and a rigid panel attached on the other. The rigid panel has incisions that carry soil and serve as plant beds. Each module is secured in place by a system of steel tracks. A built-in, drop-by-drop watering system completes the structure, ensuring the plants their required nutrients.

Keeping in mind the practical aspects of maintenance and the possibility of having to make quick substitutions, the botanical composition devised by Rogora includes easily procurable plants that have the best ability to adapt and survive in interior environments. Rapidly growing climbing and decumbent plants were chosen to build the main structure of the plant system. It includes philodendron (*Philodendron andreanum* with dark green hanging leaves with ivory veins, and *Philodendron erubescens* "Red Emerald" with shiny leaves whose color transforms from pink to dark green as it grows), ficus (*Ficus pupila*, evergreens with small oval leaves of which there are many varieties), and cissus (*Cissus antartica*, with thin leaves and green stems, and tendrils). Shrubs and carpet plants complete the composition, arranged in stains of color with different textures to enhance ornamental effect of the wall. Numerous ferns were used, including *Adiantum capillus veneris* with light green fronds of many small triangular leaves; *Adiantum venustum,* which changes color throughout the year as its fronds gradually age and go from sea-green to brown; and the more common *Nephrolepsis esaltata.*

[opposite] This plant wall system uses panels that hold small amounts of soil. The botanical composition includes various species of hanging plants including *Philodendrum andreanum.*

GRÜNE WAND SPARKASSE INGOLSTADT

Indoorlandscaping

[opposite] Three plant walls positioned on three balconies in the Ingolstadt head-quarters of the German bank Sparkasse form a continuous interior landscape.

The German design firm Indoorlandscaping, founded in 1998 by Andreas Schmidt, is made up of an interdisciplinary team of professionals. It specializes in interior design and in projecting spaces that incorporate the use of living plant matter. In 2001, Indoorlandscaping teamed with Häring Radke & Partner to develop and patent the Grüne Wand system for making plant walls. This system, like the one designed by Patrick Blanc, makes use of hydroponics to cultivate plants, vertically, in closed spaces.

The Grüne Wand is made by joining modular metal boxes which have synthetic sponge panels to support plant growth. The plant cover is made with a mix of small carpet plants (*Soleirolia soleiro-lii* for example), combined with ferns (such as *Nephrolepsis exaltata*). The containers are anchored to metal frames that serve as supports, and the entire structure, equipped with a drop-by-drop irrigation system, is only eight inches thick. A basin built into the floor at the base of the wall collects water and recirculates it. To date the compositions designed by Indoorlandscaping seem less spectacular than those made by Patrick Blanc (who uses a larger variety of botanical species). Nonetheless the Grüne Wand is still an effective option for creating a substantial green space in places normally thought of as primarily gray.

The series of plant walls in Sparkasse's new offices in Ingolstadt, Germany are arranged in a visually continuous column that cuts through the three levels of balconies overlooking the central atrium. It is an attractive installation, erected in 2005, that fits seamlessly into the building's design.

Covered by a spongy, evergreen carpet of compact plants with tiny leaves alternated with tufts of ferns, and lit by a series of colored spotlights built into the ceiling, the plant panels are like soft living sculptures. This aesthetic quality is enhanced by the environmental benefits produced by maintaining a dense biomass in a closed space (which include regulating the interior microclimate, purifying of the air, and absorbing sound). The designers also stress the positive psychological impact on employees. Seeing the pleasant green backdrops in the office improves their mood and lowers stress levels. The plant wall helps to turn the work environment into a soothing interior landscape.

[above] A detail of the fabric of the Grüne Wand in the shows the wall is composed primarily of two botanical species:

[opposite] Conceived as a living indoor sculpture, the plant wall has a minimal but effective design.

EX DUCATI
RIMINI

Mario Cucinella Architects

[opposite] Star jasmine plants, white wisteria, and shrub roses grow along the southern façade of the Ex Ducati building.

[overleaf, left] The "fracture" that breaks the building in two and the climbing plants that have begun to "scale" the façade.

[overleaf, right] The growth of the climbing plants, supported by the metal trellis, will eventually close the surface of the façade; only the glass surfaces on the ground floor will be free of plant growth.

A new office building and commercial space designed by the Italian firm Mario Cucinella Architects is located on a small lot previously occupied by a Ducati motorcycle dealership. Just outside of the busy resort town of Rimini (in Italy's Emilia-Romagna region), the building is insulated from noisy thoroughfares of traffic by arcing plant and mineral shields. According to the architects this choice of materials "expresses a desire to create a green corner in the city."

The four-story building has two wings sited in an "L" pattern that form a preliminary sketch. A clean "fracture" breaks the continuity of two rounded facades, highlighting the entrance which has been placed between the two structures, and forming a visual relationship with the network of roads that encircle the lot. Access to the upper floors, which house office space, is gained through a series of balconies behind a metal mesh façade. Mario Cucinella's environmental design called for a continuous grid of twenty-four-inch-square stainless steel cladding to be attached to three sides of the building. This grid supports climbing plants that will eventually grow to cover the metal cladding and form a vertical screen of plants (construction of the building was completed in 2007). The roots of star jasmine (*Rhynchospermum jasminoides*), a climbing evergreen with fragrant white blooms in May and June, find purchase in recessed gutters of earth that run along the length of the edges of the balconies. On one side of the structure the curve of the metal grid cladding deviates from the contour of the building, creating a pyramid shape. In a few years, after the covering of plants has developed and thickened, the building will appear to have a different shape.

[opposite] The southeast exposure of the Ex Ducati building.

[overleaf, left] The metal trellis on the southwest side of Ex Ducati does not follow the contour of the building, modifying the appearance of the structure's volume.

[overleaf, right] The balconies outside the offices have gutters of earth planted with star jasmine plants.

There are more than just aesthetic benefits from including plant material in an architectural design. Greening a façade on the street with enduring foliage forms a visual screen for the entire year, in addition to providing a natural filter from dust. In the summer, the plant cladding helps to reduce the strength of the sunlight entering the building, lowering the temperature and improving the comfort level of the tenants.

COUR DU PALAIS DU RHIN STRASBOURG

Agnès Daval

[opposite] An unconventional and inexpensive crate garden, made by arranging ordinary plastic boxes from nurseries, serves as the base for Daval's vertical garden.

The Palais du Rhin in Strasbourg is the historic home of the Hohenzollern family and is bound by a strict architectural heritage law that does not allow any structural modification or even possibly breaking ground and planting shrubs in the courtyard. Despite this law, and a limited budget, landscape architect Agnès Daval was able to make the austere inner courtyard of the palace more alive and appealing. In 1996 she turned a conventional 120-square-yard architectural void into a unique multi-colored *hortus conclusus* in which the theme of a potted garden is reinterpreted in a version that stretches vertically.

The minimal design was done by adopting an inexpensive, practical construction stratagem. A traditional four-part layout, following formal art garden tradition, is composed of a series of twenty-four-inch square green plastic crates (like those used in nurseries) that simply rest on the existing floor of the courtyard. The crates are arranged one next to the other to form four large square beds, each with sixty-four containers. Each crate is filled with two different species of carpet plants with rapidly growing foliage adapted to environments with little sun: dark-green-leaved periwinkles (*Vinca major*) with blue blooms from March to June, and light-green-leaved saxifrage with white blooms from May to July. The choice of carpet plants was carefully made considering contrasting colors, working with alternations of light and dark green foliage and with the effects produced by seasonal blooms. A simple crate garden risked being overpowered by the majestic sixty-five-foot high architectural backdrop. Agnès Daval decided not to limit the project to the

ground level and worked on conquering the vertical space as well, bedding climbing plants chosen

from two species: *Polygonum baldaschuanicum* and *Lonicera henry*, adapted to places with little sun.

A system of steel cables, attached to the floor of the courtyard and to the façade of the building,

make a sequence of flexible lightweight frames that allow the climbing plants to develop into per-

fumed, verdant filaments that stretch between the earth and sky. A rich assortment of carpet and

climbing plants available in specialized nurseries can be used to create an endless variety of botani-

cal combinations, but care must be taken in choosing plants that are not too heavy or vigorous—

their growth could compromise the integrity of the steel cables and the structure's hold. This sort

of crate garden is ideal for situations where architectural changes must be structurally non-invasive

and where one must retain the possibility of easily restoring the site to its original condition.

[above and opposite] Inspired by the children's fable *Jack and the Beanstalk*, the courtyard of the historic Strasbourg building houses climbing plants that grow along steel cables, filling the vertical space of the enclosure.

INNENHOF WESTPARK
ZURICH

Raderschall Landschaftsarchitekten

[opposite] A view of the curtain of steel cables and climbing plants that cross the internal courtyard (or *innenhof* in German), of Westpark, an office building in the Zurich-West business district.

The long, narrow courtyard of Westpark, an office building on the western edge of Zurich, was turned into a sophisticated garden with a minimalist design that stretches into the vertical dimension. The central void of the building was treated as one volume and draped with a curtain of steel cables and climbing plants that cuts longitudinally across the rectangle of air and light enclosed by the concrete and glass walls.

The texture of the curtain is characterized by Hall's honeysuckle (*Lonicera japonica*, a climbing evergreen plant with woolly leaves and cream white blooms) combined with different varieties of wisteria (*Wisteria* sp.). The plants rise upward, intertwining steel cables hooked to the ground and the thick bearing cable attached to opposite facades of the courtyard. This curtain of plants, sensitive to sun and wind, is a straightforward solution to the need for shade in the summer, and provides a screen to soften the direct sight lines between the large-windowed offices that overlook the courtyard. The horizontal plane of the garden has a formal design that emphasizes the theme of enclosure with a thick frame of hydrangea bushes (*Hydrangea* sp.) that bloom in varying shades of pink and blue. The ground is paved with green gravel stones from the Alps. Long rectangular basalt lava stone boxes fitted with wooden benches are set in sequence along the length of the park. They form a support base for the growth of the curtain's climbing plants, which live alongside a vibrant growth of herbaceous plants with a combination of *Geranium* "Johnson's Blue," *Anemone blanda,* and *Campanula* sp. In the spring and summer, when the herbaceous plants in the

boxes bloom, the garden is filled with colors ranging from bright blue to violet. In addition to the visual appeal of the tones of color, the senses are stimulated by a mix of fragrant honeysuckles and wisteria and the presence of water, made dynamic by three stone fountains in front of the benches. About one thousand square yards in size, this delightful outdoor room with minimalist poetics maintains its full aesthetic power in the winter, when the vibrantly colored blooms are replaced by monochrome greens that highlight the carefully executed design.

[above] The garden in early spring: a variety of hydrangeas frame the perimeter of the courtyard.

[opposite] A thick cable runs the length of the garden and supports a series of thinner cables that in turn support the growth of climbing plants.

[overleaf] The rectangular planters also serve as benches. During the spring and summer herbaceous plants fill the garden with colors ranging from blue to violet.

GRASS HOUSE
TOKYO

Terunobu Fujimori

[opposite] Grass and herbaceous plants are an essential part of the architectural language of Grass House.

This wood and stone construction incorporates volumes inspired by the forms from an ancient Asian building tradition and takes its name (intentionally distorted) from an icon of modern Western architecture, Philip Johnson's Glass House. Terunobu Fujimori's Grass House, designed as his own home, is a tangible manifesto of a design philosophy that opposes the principles of cerebral purity and abstractions generated by modernism (labeled the "white school" by Fujimori, referencing the color of dissected cerebral matter). He counters modernist purity with an aesthetic that favors a feeling for real everyday life (the "red school," alluding to the color of blood). In his design for the Grass House, completed in 1995, he experiments with unusual ways of integrating non-plant and plant materials, arranging containers with small dandelions and portulaca plants in gaps between the stone slabs of the external cladding.

"I continued thinking about the 'greening' of architecture. I observed various examples of this concept, ranging from Le Corbusier's proposal for a roof garden to houses covered with ivy. Based on such experiences and speculation, I came to the conclusion that a roof garden would not work, and that the right path to follow would be to actually 'green' the surfaces of walls. After pursuing this line of thought, I ended up proposing 'finishing off a skyscraper with tampopo (dandelions).' I kept thinking about the relationship between architecture, a man-made thing, and plants, which are natural. In other words, I was searching for the ideal visual relationship between them. I also wanted to avoid the concept of 'symbiosis,' a kind of buzzword in Japan at that time. This concept

seemed somewhat naive and untrue to me. Wouldn't a relationship of 'parasitism' be more real? In the great natural world, small man-made things are parasitic, whereas nature acts as a parasite on the large man-made things of cities and architecture. I knew from experience that such a scene was beautiful. What you must beware of when allowing plants to become parasites of buildings is not to deal with nature in a free and self-indulgent way. In many case, if you let greenery thrive freely on roof in order to create ecological houses, the greenery forms a separate world of beauty from the building itself, and the building and the greenery end up becoming detached. What I wanted to do was make plants grow from a building in the way soft downy hair grows out of the skin." (Terunobu Fujimori, *Y'avant-garde Architecture*, 1998).

[above and opposite] Fujimori has created a timeless architecture in the context of an urban periphery.

[overleaf] The roof as a poetic space with *Tarassacus officinalis* plants, the common dandelion. Grass House is also known as Tampopo House; *tampopo* means dandelion in Japanese.

TSUBAKI CASTLE
TOKYO

Terunobu Fujimori

[opposite] Details of the materials used—wood, stone, grass—to construct an architecture that seems to lie outside the bounds of time and space.

Crowning the roof of Terunobu Fujimori's architectural composition of inorganic and organic materials, built for a distillery of *shochu* (a traditional Japanese liquor made by fermenting grain or sweet potatoes) in 2000, is a camellia. Fujimori has declared that his "dream is to grow plants on buildings just as the human body grows hair"; accordingly the roof of Tsubaki Castle has been turned into a poetic space. Other projects by the Japanese architect incorporate signature plants—the dancing growth of leeks on Leek House, the dandelions on Green House, the young black pine tree on Pine Tree House—so it is not surprising to find a camellia, a symbol of the Japanese culture and landscape, colonizing the peak of this building. Eighteenth-century botanist Carl Linnaeus gave the scentless "Japanese rose" the name *Camellia japonica*. In 1691 German scientist Engelbert Kaempfer noted in his *Amoenitas exoticae* that the rapidly growing bush is widespread in the damp forests of Japan where it is called "tsubaki."

Plants are a constituent part of Fujimori's architectural vocabulary, and a guiding principle of his design philosophy. They are defining elements of Tsubaki Castle—the roof is punctuated with a shrub, and the exterior walls have thin strips of grass growing in the seams of the diamond-shaped pattern of stone slabs cladding each face of the central structure. Fujimori's architecture offers a fresh interpretation of modernist precepts that require architectural compositions based on the purity of simple volumes. To be sure, Tsubaki Castle is an assembly of simple volumes—a pyramid set on a cube forms the main structure, which is in turn inserted into an elongated rectangular

[opposite] The small square pavilion of Fujimori's Tsubaki Castle has a grass covered, pyramid-shaped roof and camellia (tsubaki) tree set at its peak.

base—but the independent expressive language of the work makes it a significant departure from modernism. Fujimori himself notes that "I have learned a lot from modern architecture, things such as how to handle mass or the texture of a surface. But what I make is completely different from existing modern architecture. That is why people tell me that they have never seen anything like it before." This statement bespeaks an international architecture, but one that is oriented toward reinventing vernacular ideas. His is an architectural avant-garde that references the past rather than the future, an architecture that does not seem to reference the tradition of a particular place, or belong to a specific time.

MFO PARK
ZURICH

Burckhardt+Partner, Raderschall Landschaftsarchitekten

[opposite] The metal structure that encompasses MFO Park has elevated platforms and walkways to take over the vertical dimension.

Toward the end of the nineties, the Mashcinenfabrik Oerlikon industrial center in northern Zurich was closed and an urban area of about one hundred thirty acres was set aside to build Zentrum Zürich Nord. The master plan to re-shape this portion of the city includes residential buildings, administrative centers, and shopping centers all carefully sited to create an integrated system of varying types of open public space. MFO Park, named after now defunct local machine shops, occupies a corner in this complex urban mosaic. The architectural design—a joint project by Swiss firms Burckhardt+Partner and Raderschall Landschaftsarchitekten—seeks to reinterpret the traditional public park, enhancing it by expanding the vertical dimension. Though it was opened in 2002, only the first phase of the park is complete. Even so, the park demonstrates possibilities for enriching the visual aspect of a designed urban void.

MFO Park, "the largest garden arbor in the world," has a captivating hybrid architecture, dubbed a "park-house" by its designers. The 10,000-square-yard lot is enclosed by a grand metal structure which bounds three sides of the park and rises to a height of almost sixty feet. The architects have envisioned cladding this steel skeleton with twelve hundred climbing and sarmentous plants (representing over one hundred different species). This is an exaggerated post-industrial expression of traditional architectural elements from the art of gardens: the trellis and the arbor, which are openly quoted among the design inspirations chosen by the architects. Formed by a weave of branches and wicker arranged to form a rigid lattice, the trellis has been used since

Roman times as a support for the growth of climbers, to decorate stone walls, and to serve as a divider between different areas of a garden. In MFO Park, the wood trellis has been replaced by a system of metal frames and steel cables stretched to form a long grid. The use of an all steel construction system, typical of industrial buildings, gives this novel park-building an almost harsh appearance that evokes the local industrial history.

The park stretches three stories upward. A series of ramps and suspended walkways let visitors circulate through different levels of the park and access suspended platforms. Udo Weilacher, (a professor of landscape architecture at the University of Hannover) commented that from observation platforms on the top of the "park-house" visitors are able to "enjoy the feeling that they are on the deck of a container ship stranded in the city, and look for striking landmarks in the immediate vicinity. This lofty, airy timber deck is already one of the most popular meeting places for young people in the area, and a lot of people are fascinated by the goose-pimply feeling they get when looking down into the depths through the brightly lit grid, while others are already working out the first tests for their courage on the easily accessible steel structure." The park takes on the nature of a theater set. The resonating metallic sound of footsteps on suspended walkways, the gentle diffused echo of voices and laughter, and the vibrations of the steel cables all work together to create an engaging dimension where visitors are simultaneously spectators and actors. The theme of theatricality is further developed by the varied, shifting, acrobatic nature of the structure

[above] MFO Park is the contemporary, large-scale version of the traditional wood trellis pergola used in seventeenth-century formal gardens.

[opposite] The steel skeleton of the structure is visible in the in winter.

[overleaf] Viewed from the platforms high above the park, the large open space enclosed by the metal structure looks like a theater set.

itself. Inside the grand metal and plant construction, the climbing steel cables are positioned to form a sort of colonnade. On the exterior is a thick skin of plant life that changes color, scent, and texture with the passing seasons. The landscape architects of Raderschall Landschaftsarchitekten explain that the plant structure consists of all possible varieties of climbing and sarmentous plants grown in Switzerland that are able to survive the local climate. They have been arranged according to a series of criteria, including resistance to exposure, speed of growth, and color. Particularly robust varieties of vines, wisteria, and *Fallopia* that grow quickly and that can reach of great lengths (for example, in optimal conditions wisteria climbers can grow as high as sixty-five feet) were introduced to ensure a dense cover of plants in a short period of time. Varieties of rose and honeysuckle plants, that do not grow as quickly or as high, were also planted as well as smaller plants, like clematis (*Clematis* sp.), which are fragrant and have abundant blooms and offer a strong ornamental impact. On the northeast side of the structure different varieties of ivy were used to form a dense and enduring plant façade.

MFO Park also serves as an educational tool. Steel plaques inscribed with the names of the plants placed at eye level allow any curious observer to easily identify the many botanical species found in the park. One example of the rich variety of species planted can be found on the fans of steel cables that form part of the tensile structure. These lines of metal serve as a support for a combination of climbing plants that include: *Humulus lupulus* "Hopfen," *Clematis* "Huldmine," *Vitis* coignetiae, Clematis macropetal "Pearl Rose," Rosa Paul's Himalayan Musk, Vitis vinifera var. sylvestris, Rosa "New Dawn," Fallopia aubertii, Clematis "Mrs. Cholmondeley," Clematis "Betty Corning," Clematis montana grandiflora, Lonicera periclymenum "Loly," and Parthenocissus quinquefolia.

The park is also a perfect location for concerts, plays, and outdoor cultural events. The large void enclosed by its great metal shell has been organized into two spaces with different configurations. A larger square paved with sand-colored pebbles is marked on the two long sides by an arcade of bands of steel cable wrapped by climbing plants and opens on the northeast side of the park. The space has an ample covered parterre that is also available for temporary installations. Elevated wood and steel platforms overlook this open area. A smaller rectangle of space on the opposite side of the park can serve as a lobby. This outdoor room is defined by a weathering steel stringcourse and is about four inches lower than the main floor, creating a pool-like effect. This circumscribed area, paved with loose iridescent green and blue recycled glass pebbles, sparkles beautifully in the sun. The furnishing elements are few and simple and include loosely distributed wood and steel benches and a small pool bound by a weathering steel band and encircled by water irises. A sequence of parallel lines of thick alternately shaped evergreen yew and hornbeam bushes serve as a link between the interior and exterior of the park-house. In an area saturated with post-industrial aesthetics the abstract, minimalist composition of the park-house gives it a suspended atmosphere. The theatrical nature of MFO Park is further emphasized at night when neon lights attached to the metal framework and spotlights recessed in the ground turn the park-house into a volume of bright, sparkling color.

[opposite] The "park-house" is paved with loose iridescent green and blue recycled glass pebbles.

[overleaf, left] Climbing plants with early spring sproutings.

[overleaf, right] The unique steel cable and climbing plant colonnade bounds the central empty space of the park.

QUAI BRANLY MUSEUM PLANT WALL
PARIS

Jean Nouvel, Patrick Blanc

[opposite] The façade of the museum is composed of glass, iron, and plant life.

In Paris even the most distracted passersby notice the one thousand square yards of lush plants covering the front of a forty-foot tall building. Part of the Quai Branly Museum designed by Jean Nouvel, the exceptional success this variegated plant façade is yet another of Patrick Blanc's botanical accomplishments. Construction of the plant wall, started during the summer of 2004, involved arranging over fifteen thousand plants. This living botanical catalogue includes one hundred fifty different species from Japan, China, the United States, and central Europe. The green cladding turns this architectural project into an outsized example of "artificial nature," an urban façade—colonized by an expansive variety of herbaceous plants and shrubbery—transformed into the face of a magnificent verdant cliff.

Nouvel noted that this museum is "a place marked by the symbols of the forest, the river, and obsessions with death and oblivion. It is a place where asylum is given to works censored or disdained that originated in Australian and American lands. It is a charged and inhabited place, in a dialogue with the ancestral spirits of people who, having discovered the human condition, have invented divinities and faiths. It is a unique, strange place. Poetic and unsettling." The architect described the design of the museum as a new container and an emblem of the "other arts." The museum is more like a territory within the urban landscape of Paris than a building. More specifically, it is a frontier to be explored, a dynamic space dedicated to the coming together of different cultures and civilizations. The museum is dedicated to presenting arts from outside the European

tradition. In addition to new acquisitions the museum holds diverse collections of artworks and objects that had been housed in the now closed Musée des Arts Africains et Océaniens and from the ethnographic department of the Musée de l'Homme. The catalogue of works now assembled includes ancient objects of archeological and anthropological value as well as pieces by contemporary artists.

The museum complex takes up a five acre lot between Rue de l'Université and Quai Branly, along the bank of the Seine. The arrangement of its four buildings, Bâtiment Musée, Bâtiment Branly, Bâtiment de l'Université, and Bâtiment Auvent—ou Samouraï, is intended to generate a feeling of progressive discovery for the visitor. The glass curtain wall along the Quai Branly, Patrick Blanc's plant wall, the interior garden, and the large colored horn-like boxes set in the façade of the Bâtiment Musée serve as a sequence of perceptual thresholds and symbolic elements.

The plant wall covers the northern wall of Bâtiment Branly, which holds administrative offices and a theater. Aligned with the wall of a neighboring nineteenth-century Haussmann-style building, the iron, glass, and plant-life façade proceeds straight for about one hundred feet and then arcs toward the interior of the site where it connects with the Bâtiment Auvent—ou Samouraï. This curved arc defines the depth of the building and creates a spatial connection between the vertical garden designed by Blanc and the horizontal garden by Gilles Clément. The later garden is a gentle undulating space filled with symbolic references evoking animist and polytheist cosmologies. The

[above and opposite] The plant wall of the Quai Branly Museum in the urban context of Paris.

[overleaf] The building wears the plant-life façade like a primitive mask.

[opposite] This corner of the Bâtiment Auvent–ou Samouraï is where Patrick Blanc's vertical garden and Gilles Clément's horizontal garden intersect.

figurative and conceptual partnership between these two sections amplifies the sensation that the museum is a forest in the city. Nouvel sought to make a museum that is "a refuge without a façade, in a woods."

After visiting the museum and its collections, viewing the Bâtiment Branly from the street conjures the impression that the plant cladding is worn by the building like an unusual primitive mask, the mark of an archaic culture. This impression is emblematic of the semantic and symbolic connection between Blanc's work and the contents of the museum. Blanc himself explains that in choosing the plant species, he favored plants with brownish tinges to evoke the colors and materials of the works of art from tropical places, traditionally made of wood, mud, and adobe.

[left] Taking advantage of the various physical characteristics of the plants used in his compositions, Blanc is able to create sculptural compositions.

[opposite] The plant wall introduces a change of pace into the daily urban scene.

[overleaf] A few plants with brown and deep-red-colored leaves (like l'*Heuchera* sp. and l'*Aiuga* sp.) evoke the colors and materials of the handmade works in the museum's collection.

FLOWER TOWER
PARIS

Edouard François

[opposite] Large pots containing bamboo plants are incorporated in the structure of Flower Tower's balconies.

Flower Tower is a garden-house, a ten-story building with thirty apartments designed by Edouard François. It is a simple architectural volume that follows the "green over gray" motto coined by Emilio Ambasz. Located on the eastern edge of Paris, this white, gray, and green monolith is sited in the sunniest part of a park that forms part of the connective fabric of a new residential district built to the master plan of architect Christian de Portzamparc. Hundreds of large white cement flowerpots, containing bamboo plants, are arranged in orderly rows along the building's regular terraces. These plants have been incorporated into the building's outer skin to create a unique façade. Flower Tower follows the doctrine of growing domestic greenery that is adapted to urban apartment life. François relates that while he was walking through Paris he noticed people's desire for nature in the city. "Almost every balcony has plants. One could even say that balconies are only used for this purpose, for filtering out the city and minimizing the effect of urban density. There is a heroic aspect to these small gardens because the balconies were never intended to serve this purpose. They do not have faucets for watering and the pots must be carried up one by one, not to mention the cost of the plants in city garden centers... one never has enough money to buy pots and plants, and together they are too big and heavy to transport. Finally the biggest problem remains watering the plants."

Flower Tower is a vertical expression of the theme of small, private city gardens. The residents of the building are not obligated to look after the plants; an automatic system, which collects

rainwater from the terraces, gives the plants their needed supply of water and fertilizers through tubes set in the concrete platforms. In this age of "techno-nature," it seems that this vertical garden is able to live autonomously. The design allows the plants live together with the building, forming a symbiotic relationship between the two. For the residents of Flower Tower, the voluntary act of growing plants on a terrace has become a forced choice. The plants that run along the exterior of Flower Tower are an essential element of the architectural image conceived by the architect. In addition to the two bamboo plants that were planted in each of the three hundred eighty giant pots, each apartment is also supplied with an empty pot to hold plants chosen by the owner.

[above and opposite] Constructed in 2004, Flower Tower is located in a mixed development zone in Porte d'Asnières in the seventeenth *arrondissement* of Paris.

[overleaf] The flower pots and bamboo are essential parts of this white and gray monolith's architectural image, even though some of the plants have not taken root.

L'IMMEUBLE QUI POUSSE
MONTPELLIER

Edouard François

[opposite] The boxy volumes and unique façade of L'immeuble qui pousse harmonize with the surrounding trees.

It is difficult not to notice the seven-story two hundred fifty-foot long apartment complex that stands in the middle of a park along the banks of the Les river in Montpellier. The visual impact of Edouard François's experimental design is striking. Using the local landscape as a point of reference, and adopting the concepts of growth and change as driving principles of the design, the exterior of the building was turned into a rocky garden.

Resting on a ballast of massive blocks of stone (some of which weigh over eleven tons) the façade of the building is made of overlapping prefabricated gabions, similar to those used for landscape engineering projects (building river banks for example). The gabions are filled with a collection of inert materials—lava stone pebbles from Turkey, a porous stone material like pumice stone, and fertilized earth—held in place by a stainless steel mesh. Also inside the gabions are more than ten tons of *Sedum* sp. seeds. *Sedum* are plants from the *Crassulacee* family, which grow easily and spontaneously among pebbles and rocks or at the base of walls. Their botanical name (from the Latin *sedare* = to calm) stems from the ancient Roman habit of growing the plant on the roofs of houses; it was believed that the plant served as natural lightning shield.

Inside the structure of L'immeuble qui pousse is an automatic irrigation system that runs between the gabions. Activated for one hour every night, the system supplies the seeds with the proper amount of water and nutrients to sprout and grow. The structure also requires a suitable drainage system that is carefully designed to prevent moisture from entering into the

apartments. Very slowly over time, the building has started to change its skin with the growth and spread of the *Sedum* plants between the gaps in the rocky façade. It is the changing character this unusual porous and sensitive coating, playfully called "Frankenstein skin" by François, that characterizes L'immeuble qui pousse. The overall image is that of a refuge or home with archaic features.

According to François there were two key themes in the design from the start: the balconies and the construction materials. The balconies are a prerequisite for all the residential buildings in the local urban development program. In the design of L'immeuble qui pousse the distribution and inclusion of balconies was decisive, to the point that according to François the project might have been called "the balcony, in all its forms." The theme is variously expressed with ceaseless creativity. As François explains, there are "balcony gardens for eating with friends, balcony-cabins perched among nearby trees in order to become more familiar with them, planar balconies with views, for the curious, of the foliage, and terrace balconies that seem to be homes." The large "balcony-cabins," measuring about one hundred sixty square feet, resemble wooden shoeboxes without lids. They were conceived as private spaces amidst the branches of trees and serve as outdoor rooms, extending the living area of the apartment. To emphasize the impression that these balcony-cabins are tree houses, many of them are supported by a system of gold-colored steel columns and connected to the building via a wood walkway. There are also smaller

[above and opposite] Variations on the theme of balconies including "balcony-cabins" supported by colored steel columns, "balcony-cabins" attached to the face of the building, and planar concrete balconies with wood fencing serving as railings.

188

[opposite] This corner of the building highlights the play of volumes and materials that define the building's architecture.

[above] The apartment complex stands behind a curtain of plane trees.

balconies; simple rectangular projecting planes in reinforced concrete with wooden fencing similar to that often used at seashores to divide sections of the beach.

The second key theme, the materials selection, is closely connected to the concept of the building's skin, conceived by the architect as a context-sensitive membrane "with trees standing as sentries, as if they were along the banks of a river, guarding against summertime temperatures. It must ensure the comfort and (in)visibility of the building." In other words, it is both a living cladding exposed to the elements and a protective camouflage covering.

[opposite] Wooden balconies that resemble lidless shoeboxes function as outdoor living rooms.

[right] Projecting through the branches is a refuge that would have been to the liking of the tree-climbing nobleman in Italo Calvino's *Baron in the Trees*.

[overleaf] Filled with lava stone from Turkey and soil, the rocky surface of the walls are intended to become gradually covered with the *Sedum* plants sown inside the gabions. The façades are also fertile terrain for the spontaneous growth of carpeting and climbing species.

ACROS BUILDING
FUKUOKA

Emilio Ambasz

[opposite] A view of the ACROS Building, also known as the Fukuoka Prefectural International Hall, from the park at the foot of the building. The green space of the park extends vertically onto the edifice.

Emilio Ambasz has been described as an iconoclastic architect with a sense of wonder and as a tireless inventor of metaphors. He is also a pioneer of green architecture. In his work, a sense of place, technological experimentation, ecological concerns, and symbolism combine to give shape to buildings in which the landscape becomes the primary figurative point of reference. Ambasz's visionary projects speak a language that is simultaneously new and old, integrating natural materials (plants, water, wind) with architectural structure. His projects are hyper-natural constructions where, on the local level, form is given to the desire to actively resist the progressive process of the depletion of environmental resources on a planetary scale.

Completed in 1995, the ACROS Building may be the best known expression of his design philosophy founded on the concept of green architecture. Ambasz has been dedicated to the practical application of this philosophy, summed up by the simple motto "green over gray," since the seventies. The ACROS Building is a fifteen-story cultural and exhibition center that vertically expands the dimensions of a park at the foot of the building with a system of terraces and hanging gardens covered with luxuriant plant life. The façade-garden is open to the public. Visitors are free to venture on a vertical walk amidst the greenery, taking one of the series of ramps and stairs that connect all the terraces. One can sit and rest in one of the gardens, lie on a field of grass on the roof, or simply enjoy the extraordinary panoramic view of the city. It is difficult not to think of the building as a contemporary version of the mythical Tower of Babel or the legendary Hanging Gardens

of Babylon. In addition to generating an array of metaphorical and symbolic meanings, the design of the ACROS Building is a practical example of how to reconcile private economic business interests (tied to the use of available buildable land) and the public desire for open public space and greenery in urban environments. The ACROS Building can be viewed as a precursor to a broader vision of a "green town"—not a return to the idea of a picturesque bucolic garden city, but rather a new urban landscape that allows for the possibility of a house and a garden on equal terms (instead of the house reigning over the garden). In 2000 Ambasz noted that "There is a philosophic question here: we have to redefine what is nature and what is man-made nature. In a situation such as the global one, certainly exacerbated in Japan, where a tree exists either because someone planted it or because someone decided to leave it there, it is imperative that we create a new definition of what is meant by man-made nature. Such a definition would have to incorporate and expand not only the creation of gardens and public spaces but also the creation of architecture which must be seen as one specialized aspect of the making of man-made nature."

[above] The Ambasz's ziggurat co-exists with Fukuoka's dense urban fabric; it is an overt expression of his visionary "green over gray" philosophy.

[opposite] The sequence of verdant terraces and flowering cherry trees in the park create contrasting patterns in the spring.

[overleaf] For Emilio Ambasz, to build with nature is to use nature as an "aesthetic-biological support for artifice."

[left and opposite] The terrace gardens
arranged on the face of the ACROS Building
are connected by a system of ramps and
stairways. Thirty-five thousand plants grow
in fourteen-level garden.

[overleaf, left and right] The building was
conceived as a vertical extension of an
existing public park.

SPORTPLAZA MERCATOR
AMSTERDAM

Venhoeven CS Architecten, Copijn

[opposite] A side view of the Sportplaza Mercator with a mixture of cladding.

Adding a built volume to a public park is a delicate operation, particularly if the park in question has historic value and is treasured by locals. Rembrandtpark is a large scenic park on the western edge of Amsterdam frequented by tourists and residents alike. The park's administration decided to launch an architectural competition for the commission to build a new athletic complex, Sportplaza Mercator. The winning design had to be a structure that would merge into the context of the park. Dutch studio Venhoeven CS won the competition with a building that boasts a hybrid architecture, almost entirely covered by a layer of plants. The building's low but complex volume holds a gym, three swimming pools, a restaurant, and a café. The exterior and roof of the structure are covered by a porous skin of roughly fifty thousand plants including small shrubs and carpet plants. A wall of glass—allowing passersby to see one of the swimming pools inside, blurring the relationship between the interior and exterior space—is the only part of the exterior surface that escapes the colonization of plant life.

The Wonderwall system, developed by the Copijn landscape architecture studio in Utrecht, was used to build Sportplaza Mercator's plant walls. The structure of this system is built from modular elements; each element is composed of three layers: a steel mesh that is anchored to the building, a shielding plate attached to the inside of the mesh, and a thin external pane. This outside layer consists of a metal frame and a felt-covered plastic panel with regularly placed slots where plants in containers are inserted. An automated irrigation system is built into the plant walls allow-

ing the plants to grow in nutrient enriched water, hydroponically, without further care. Differing from the more flexible system patented by Patrick Blanc (where the plants are placed directly into pockets made of felt, allowing for a more varied repertoire of compositions and designs) the Wonderwall system has a more rigid, geometric scheme. Nonetheless the variation of colors and textures obtained by combining different botanical species renders the final visual effect just as striking. Careful consideration of the orientation of the various facades, assessing the exposure to the sun, informed the selection and distribution of the species of plants used. Sportplaza Mercator opened in 2006 and in 2007 it won the Dutch National Building Prize and the Mies van der Rohe Award.

[above] The building, located on an edge of Rembrandtpark in Amsterdam, is an element of transition between the fabric of the city and the fabric of the park.

[opposite] A wall of windows along the street front renders the interior of the sports facility visible to passersby.

[overleaf] The complex shape of the building is almost completely clad with plants.

[second overleaf] The doors and windows are like wedges inserted in the continuity of the green covering.

[opposite and right] Young plants are inserted into slits in the felt-covered panel creating a regular pattern of vegetation on the cladding of the building.

Z58
SHANGHAI

Kengo Kuma

[opposite] Stacked ribbons of metal and cascading ivy plants define the front façade of Kengo Kuma's Z58.

An unusual urban façade can be found in a residential area of central Shanghai at 58 Panyu Road. The Chun-Tai Lighting Corporation, a lighting system design and manufacturing concern, asked Japanese architect Kengo Kuma to project an addition to their headquarters and showroom. The resulting modifications expanded the original three-story building, which once housed a watch factory during the Cultural Revolution, with the addition of a fourth floor and the introduction of a large atrium. Finished in 2006, the new volume known as "Z58" is defined by the striking elevation that faces the street. This front is composed of stacked steel elements, a sequence of shining straight parallel bands that create a rhythmic alternation of voids and solids. This façade serves as a protective filter between the street and the interior of the building. The scenic character of the façade is characterized by the growth of orderly lines of thick ivy along the top of each of the bands of metal that bedeck the front of the building. The falling shoots and dark leaves of the plants temper the reflective quality of the steel and create a beguiling play of forms and colors. The mirrored images of the plants seem to suggest a total integration between natural and non-natural elements. Based on a simple geometry, the minimal composition of the façade revolves around the relationships between light, space, and materials.

[above and opposite] According to the architect "our immediate task is to adapt the pastoral and artisanal technologies of gardening to our complex and difficult world."

[overleaf] Abrupt changes in scale and architectural style can be seen in the array of buildings along Panyu Road in Shanghai.

[left] Clean construction details and straightforward design are part of Kengo Kuma's architectural language.

[opposite] Detail of the ivy-filled containers and the reflective metal surface.

[overleaf] The iridescent façade creates variations of light and color that follow the rhythms of the day. The play of reflections is particularly visible as daylight fades.

PARADISE PARK CHILDREN'S CENTRE
LONDON

DSDHA, Marie Clark, Alan Conisbee

[opposite] The main façade of the Paradise Park Children's Centre has been designed to support a vertical garden.

The plant façade of the Paradise Park Children's Centre in Islington is the result of a partnership between the London-based architectural design firm DSDHA, landscape architect Marie Clark, and engineer Alan Conisbee. Commissioned by IGS (Islington Green Space, a mixed public and private agency responsible for managing local open spaces and their facilities) and located in a public park in a residential district north of London, the building was designed applying principles of environmentally sustainable architecture.

The plant walls were constructed using steel lattices, roughly sixteen inches square, attached to the face of the building. Within this welded framework are panels that support the growth of the plants. The selection of plants that make up the botanical composition of the walls includes thirty species including carpet, climbing, and shrub plants. A total of seventy thousand plants were placed in the walls and they are regularly watered by a built-in automatic irrigation system that is supplied with rainwater collected in a tank on the roof of the building.

Sited at the edge of the large open expanse, the architects chose to develop the design of the center following a design strategy that would allow them to insert a "garden-building" in the context of the park. The abundant plant walls on three sides of the building render the structure and its immediate surroundings into an evocative setting. Before the center's realization, the park had been described as being closer to a motorcycle junkyard than to an earthly "paradise." The building of this community center—which houses a children's center, a day care center, a café, and

offices—triggered the re-development of the entire park. In December 2006, the Paradise Park Children's Centre won a "Partners in Excellence" award from Sure Start, a British government program that seeks to improve services for children.

[above] The metal lattice, an integral part of the building's green cladding, is clearly visible.

[opposite] The lush botanical composition includes a selection of begonias: *Bergenia* "Ballawley," *Bergenia Cordifolia* "Purpurea," *Pelargonium* sp., and ferns.

[overleaf] The building blends in with the context of the park.

[left and opposite] The careful selection of vegetation used—perennial herbaceous plants and small shrubs—produces variations in blooms, scents, and colors year round.

BIBLIOGRAPHY

Criticism and Fiction

Barthes, Roland, *L'empire des signes* (Geneva, Editions d'Art Albert Skira, 1970); *Empire of Signs* (Farrar Straus and Giroux, 1982).

Calvino, Italo, *La foresta-radice-labirinto* (*The Forest-Root-Labyrinth*) (Milan, Mondadori, 1981).

D'Angelo, Paolo, *Estetica della natura: Bellezza naturale, paesaggio, arte ambientale* (*Aesthetics of Nature: The Beauty of Nature, Landscape, and Ambient Art*) (Rome-Bari, Laterza, 2001).

The Art of Landscape and the Architecture of Gardens

Amidon, Jane, *Radical Landscapes: Reinventing Outdoor Space* (London, Thames & Hudson, 2001).

Beardsley, John, *Earthworks and Beyond: Contemporary Art in the Landscape* (New York, Cross River Press, 1984).

Hill, Penelope, *Jardins d'aujourd'hui en Europe: Entre art et architecture* (Antwerp, Fonds Mercator, 2002); *Contemporary History of Garden Design: European Gardens Between Art and Architecture* (Basel, Birkhäuser, 2004).

Mosser, Monique, Teyssot, George (ed.), *L'architettura dei giardini d'Occidente dal Rinascimento al Novecento* (Milan, Electa 1990); *The Architecture of Western Gardens: A Design History from the Renaissance to the Present Day* (Cambridge, The MIT Press, 1991).

Schroeder, Thies, *Changes in Scenery: Contemporary Landscape Architecture in Europe* (Basel, Birkhäuser, 2001).

Vercelloni, Virgilio, *Atlante storico dell'idea di giardino europeo* (*Historic Altas of European Garden Design*) (Milan, Jaca Book, 1990).

Vezzosi, Alessandro (ed.), *Il giardino d'Europa* (*The European Garden*) (Florence, Mazzotta, 1986).

Warren, William, *The Tropical Garden* (London, Thames & Hudson, 1991).

Weilacher, Udo, *Between Landscape Architecture and Land Art* (Basel, Birkhäuser, 1996).

Weilacher, Udo, *In Gardens: Profiles of Contemporary European Landscape Architecture*, (Basel, Birkhäuser, 2005).

Contemporary Art and Architecture, Green Architecture

Aymonino, Aldo (ed.) Mosco, Valerio Paolo (ed.), *Spazi pubblici contemporanei: Architettura a volume zero* (Milan, Skira, 2006); *Contemporary Public Space: Un-volumetric Architecture* (Milan, Skira, 2006)

Ambasz, Emilio, *Emilio Ambasz: The Poetics of the Pragmatic* (New York, Rizzoli International Publications, 1988).

Cooper, Paul, *Gardens Without Boundaries* (London, Mitchell Beazley, 2003).

Cooper, Paul, *Living Sculpture* (London, Mitchell Beazley, 2001).

Fagone, Vittorio (ed.), *Art in Nature* (Milan, Mazzotta, 1996).

Fujimori, Terunobu, *Y'Avant-garde Architecture*, (Tokyo, Gallery–MA books, 1998).

Gauzin-Mueller, Dominique, *Architettura sostenibile – 29 esempi di edifici e insediamenti ad alta qualità ambientale* (Milan, Edizioni Ambiente, 2003); *Sustainable Architecture and Urbanism: Design, Construction, Examples* (Basel, Birkhäuser, 2002).

Gregory, Paola, *La dimensione paesaggistica dell'architettura nel progetto contemporaneo*, (*The Dimension of Landscape in Contemporary Architectural Projects*) (Roma-Bari, Laterza, 1998).

Kastner, Jeffery, Wallis, Brian, *Land and Environmental Art* (London, Phaidon, 1998).

Koons, Jeff, *The Jeff Koons Handbook* (New York, Rizzoli International Publications, 1992).

Kuma, Kengo, "Giardinaggio versus Architettura" in *Lotus*, no. 97 (Italy, 1998).

Lloyd Jones, David, *Atlante di bioarchitettura* (Turin, UTET, 2002); *Architecture and the Environment: Contemporary Bioclimatic Buildings* (London, Laurence King Publishing, 1998).

Martin, Jean Marie "Griffe su griffe. Herzog & de Meuron a Tokyo per Prada" in *Casabella* no. 714 (Milan, Electa, 2003), pp. 78–80.

Musée du quai Branly, *L'esprit du lieu* (*The Spirit of Place*) (Paris, Editions Scala, 2006).

Omodeo Salè, Serena, *Architettura & Natura* (*Architecture & Nature*) (Milan, Mazzotta, 1994).

Prestinenza Puglisi, Luigi, *Forme e ombre* (*Forms and Shadows*) (Turin, Testo e Immagine, 2000).

Restany, Pierre (ed.), *Arte Ambientale* (*Ambient Art*) (Turin, Allemandi Editore, 1994).

Yeang, Ken, *The Green Skyscraper: The Basis for Designing Sustainable Intensive Buildings* (Munich, Prestel, 2000).

Yeang, Ken, *Ecodesign: A Manual for Ecological Design* (San Francisco, William Stout Architectural Books, 2006).

Green Roofs, Plant Walls, and Vertical Gardens

Bellomo, Antonella, *Pareti verdi* (*Green Walls*) (Naples, Gruppo Editoriale Esselibri, 2003).

Dunnett, Nigel, Kingsbury, Noel, *Planting Green Roofs and Living Walls* (London, Timber Press, 2004).

Gagnor, Riccardo, *Tetto verde* (*Green Roof*) (Milan, Be-Ma editrice, 1991).

Johnston, Jacklyn, Newton, John, *Building Green: A Guide to Using Plants on Roofs, Walls and Pavements* (London, Greater London Authority, 2004).

Poli, Tiziana, "Architettura... in vegetale" in *Modulo* no. 319 (Italy, 2006), pp. 274–280.

Botanical Aspects

Blanc, Patrick, *Être plante à l'ombre des forêts tropicales* (*Plants in the Shade of Tropical Forests*) (Paris, Nathan, 2002).

Blanc, Patrick, *Le bonheur d'être plante* (*The Well-Being of Plants*) (Paris, Maren Sell Editeurs, 2005).

Blanc, Patrick, *Folies végétales* (*Plant Follies*) (Paris, Editions du Chêne, 2006).

Cushnie, John, *Ground Cover: A Thousand Beautiful Plants for Difficult Places* (London, Kyle Cathie Limited, 1999).

Fearneley-Whittingstall, Jane, *Garden Plants Made Easy* (London, Phoenix Illustrated, 1998).

Moody, Mary, *Flowers by Colour,* (London, Weldon Russell, 1990).

Pizzetti, Ippolito, *Enciclopedia dei Fiori e del Giardino* (*Encyclopedia of Flowers and the Garden*) (Milan, Garzanti, 1998).

The Royal Horticultural Society, *Perennials* (London, Dorling Kindersley, 1996).

PHOTO CREDITS